# ESTATE PUBL

# OXFORD · ABINGD

## BEGBROKE · WOODSTOCK · EYNSHA
## KIDLINGTON · HORSPATH · WHEATL

ROAD MAP
ENLARGED TOWN CENTRE        Page 3
INDEX TO STREETS        Pages 27-32

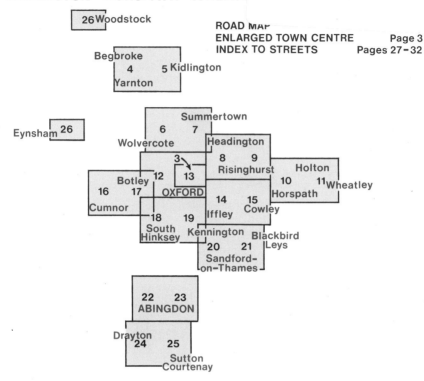

26 Woodstock

Begbroke
4    5 Kidlington
Yarnton

Eynsham 26

Summertown
6    7
Wolvercote    Headington
3
12    13    Risinghurst    Holton
Botley    10    11 Wheatley
16    17    OXFORD    Horspath
Cumnor    14    15
Cowley
18    19    Iffley
South    Kennington    Blackbird
Hinksey    20    21 Leys
Sandford-
on-Thames

22    23
ABINGDON

Drayton
24    25
Sutton
Courtenay

Every effort has been made to verify the
accuracy of information in this book
but the publishers cannot accept
responsibility for expense or loss caused
by any error or omission. Information
that will be of assistance to the user of
the maps will be welcomed.

The representation of a road, track or
footpath on the maps in this atlas is no
evidence of the existence of a right of way.

| | |
|---|---|
| One-way Street | ← |
| Car Park | ℗ |
| Place of Worship | + |
| Post Office | ● |
| Public Convenience | Ⓒ |
| Pedestrianized | ▨ |

Scale of street plans: 4 inches to 1 mile
Unless otherwise stated

Street plans prepared and published by ESTATE PUBLICATIONS, Bridewell House,
TENTERDEN, KENT, and based upon the ORDNANCE SURVEY mapping with the
permission of The Controller of H. M. Stationery Office.

The publishers acknowledge the co-operation of the local
authorities of towns represented in this atlas.

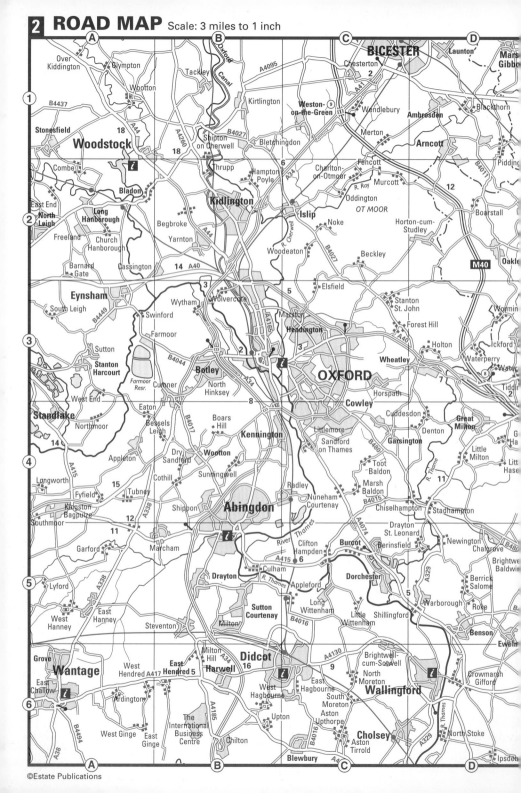

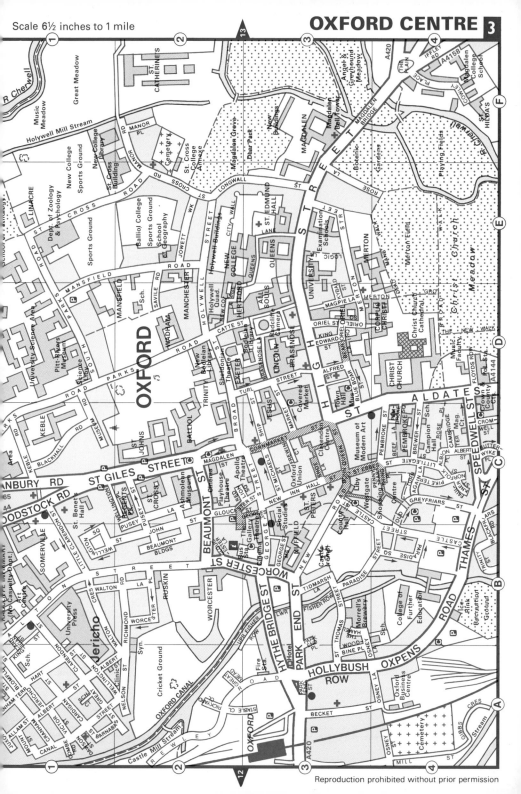

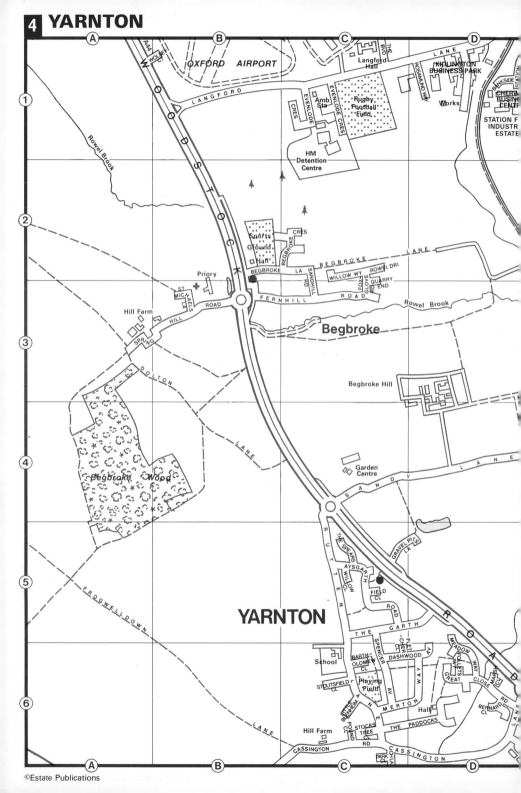

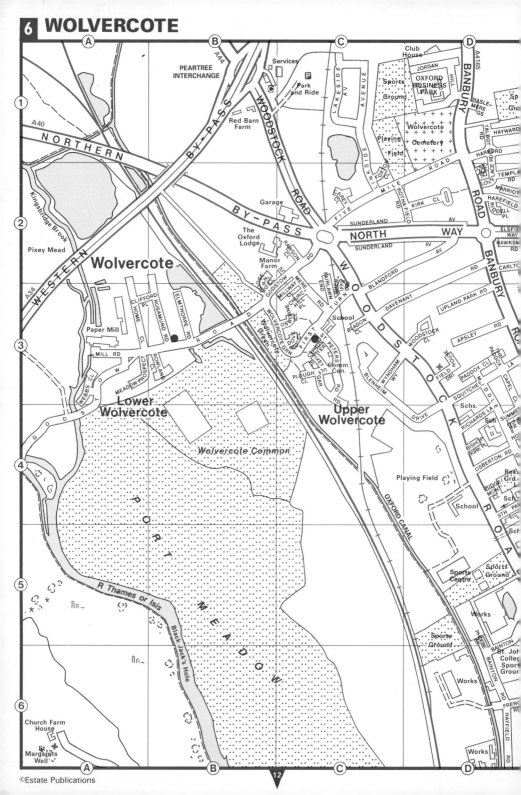

A · B · C · D

**1**

A44

PEARTREE
INTERCHANGE

Services

Park
and Ride

Club
House

Sports
Ground

JORDAN
HILL

OXFORD
BUSINESS
PARK

A4165

BANBURY

Sp
Gro

A40

NORTHERN

Red Barn
Farm

WOODSTOCK ROAD

LAKESIDE AV

AVENUE

LINKSIDE

Wolvercote
Cemetery

Playing
Field

HASLE-
MERE
GS

TALBOT

HAYWARD

**2**

Kingsbridge Brook

Pixey Mead

WESTERN

A34

BY-PASS

BY-PASS

Garage

The
Oxford
Lodge

Manor
Farm

SUNDERLAND

NORTH    WAY

SUNDERLAND AV

AV

FIVE

MILE

CAREY

FOXTON

ROTHA FIELD

KIRK CL

RD

HAREFIELD
RODELL
PL

ELSFIE
WAY

HAWKSM
CARLTO

BANBURY ROAD

**Wolvercote**

Paper Mill

MILL RD

CLIFFORD
HOME

ROSMUND RD

ELMTHORPE RD

WEBBS CL

MEADOW PROSPECT

ROWLAND

GODSTOW

MILLWAY

GODSTOW ROAD

CHURCH LA

WOLVERCOTE GN

Wolvercote
Green

FIRST TURN

RAWSON

FAIRLAWN
END

WOODSTOCK

BLANDFORD

DAVENANT

UPLAND PARK RD

APSLEY

WOODSTOCK
CL

FIELD

PADDOX CL

PADDOX
LA

CAPEL
C

SQUITCHEY
LA

RICHARDS LA

BISHOP
KIRK

OSBERTON RD

**3**

**Lower
Wolvercote**

School

St PETERS RD

BLADON CL

Comm.
Cen.

PLOUGH
CL

BLENHEIM

WYNDHAM
WY

**Upper
Wolvercote**

DRIVE

Schs.

Sch

SUMME

HO

Bee
Grd
Sch

HO

**4**

Playing Field

School

STH
PA
Sch

**Wolvercote Common**

PORT

OXFORD CANAL

ROAD

BIDGE
MONT
CL

**5**

R Thames or Isis

MEADOW

Black Jack's Hole

Sports
Centre

Sports
Ground

Works

BAINTON

St. Jol
Colleg
Spor
Grour

**6**

Church Farm
House

St.
Margarets
Well

Sports
Ground

Works

FRENC

HAYFIELD

Works

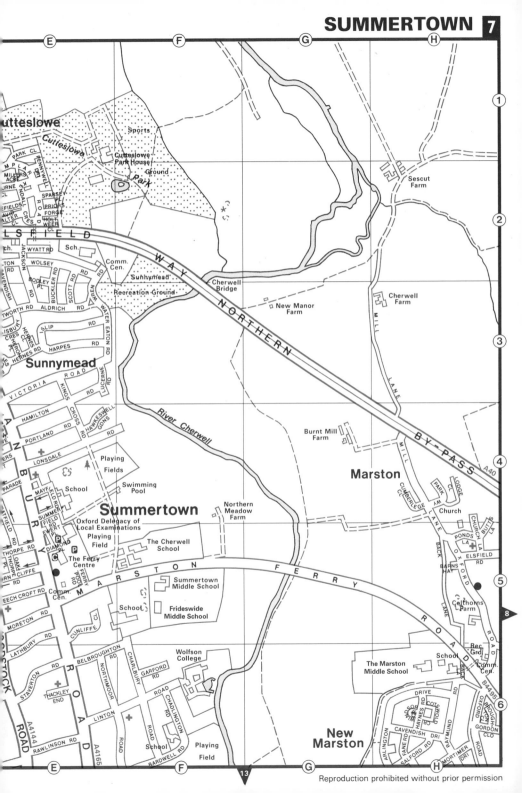

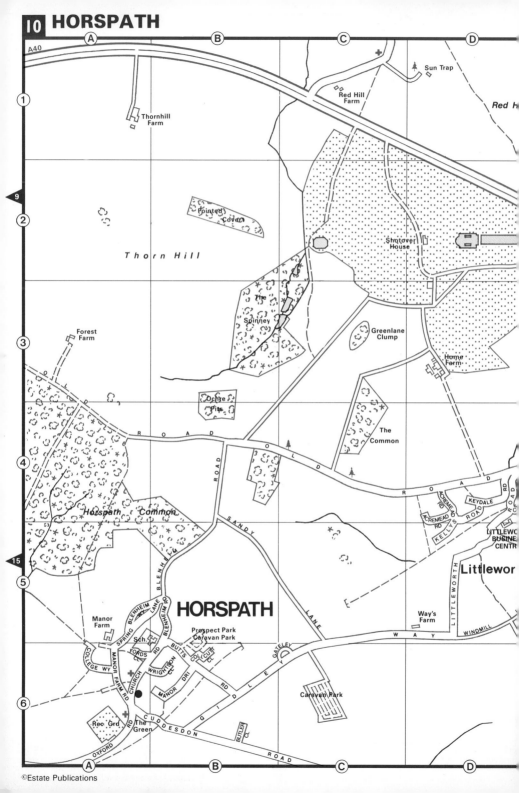

A40

A · B · C · D

1

9

2

Thornhill Farm

Red Hill Farm

Sun Trap

Red H

Thorn Hill

Pointed Covert

Shotover House

3

Forest Farm

The Spinney

Greenlane Clump

Home Farm

Ochre Pits

ROAD

OLD

The Common

4

ROAD

ROAD

ACREMEAD RD

KEYDALE

RD

ACREMEAD RD

KELLYS RD

LITTLEWO BUSINE CENTR

Horspath Common

SANDY

15

LITTLEWORTH

Littlewor

5

BLENHEIM RD

LANE

GATELEY

Way's Farm

WINDMILL

Manor Farm

Prospect Park Caravan Park

**HORSPATH**

SPRING BLENHEIM LANE

BLENHEIM RD

Sch.

BUTTS

COLCUTT CL

WAY

COLLEGE WY

FORDS CL

WRIGHTSON CL

MANOR DRI

RD

GIDLEY

Caravan Park

6

MANOR FARM RD

CHURCH

RD

Rec Grd

The Green

CUDDESDON

BUTLER CL

ROAD

OXFORD

A · B · C · D

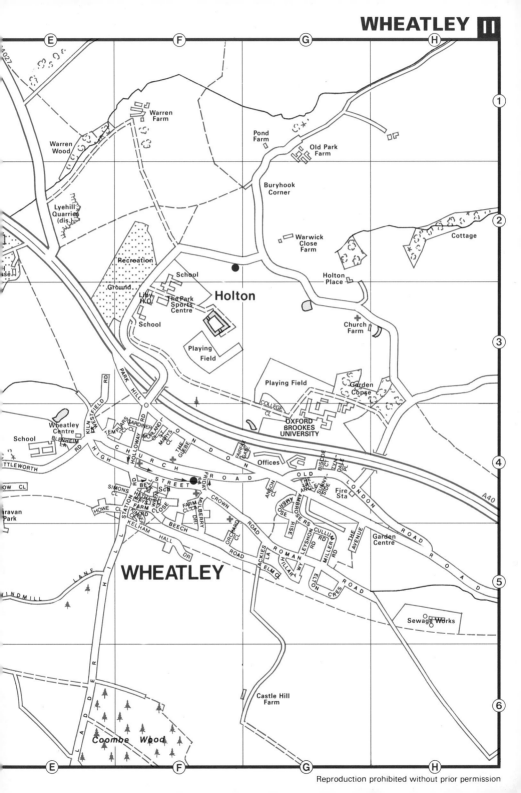

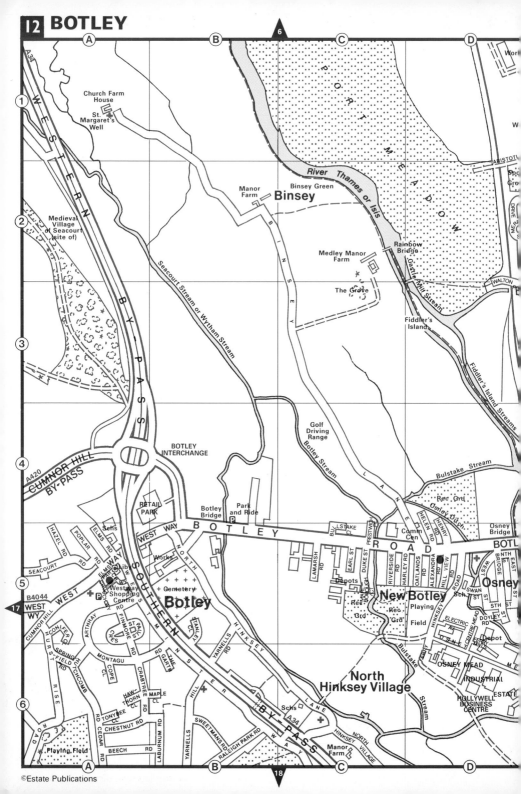

A B 6 C D

1

Church Farm House
St. Margaret's Well

WESTERN

2

Medieval Village of Seacourt (site of)

BY-PASS

3

Seacourt Stream or Wytham Stream

Manor Farm
Binsey
Binsey Green
River Thames or Isis

P O R T   M E A D O W

ARISTOTL

W

Medley Manor Farm

The Grove

Rainbow Bridge

Castle Mill Stream

Fiddler's Island

WALTON

DRIVE

Fiddler's Island Streams

4

A420
CUMNOR HILL BY-PASS

BOTLEY INTERCHANGE

Golf Driving Range

Botley Stream

Bulstake Stream

Rec. Grd.

Osney Ditch

Osney Bridge

RETAIL PARK

Botley Bridge
Park and Ride

WEST WAY
B O T L E Y
R O A D
BOTL

Comm. Cen

Osney

5

SEACOURT
B4044 WEST WY

Schs
ELMS RD
HAZEL RD
POPLAR RD
ELMS RD

WEST WAY
NORTH

Works

Westway Shopping Centre
Library
Cemetery

Botley

SOUTHERN

LAMARSH RD
EARL ST
DUKE ST
RIVERSIDE
HARLEY RD
OATLANDS
ALEXANDRA
HILL VIEW

Depots
Res. Grd

New Botley
Rec Grd
Playing Field

HELEN ST
PRESTWICH
BRIDGE RD
WEST
EAST ST
BRIDGE
NTH

SWAN
Sch ST
STH ST

Osney
ME

17
WEST WY

A420

CONF RD
HURST RISE RD
SPRINGFIELD RD
HITCHCOMB RD

MONTAGU RD
COPE
ST MARYS RD
FINMERE RD
ARTHRAY RD
CRABTREE RD
STANLEY CL
YARNELLS RD
HINKSEY
YARNELLS RD

DOYLEY RD
ELECTRIC AV
CENTRE MEAD
Depot

OSNEY
OSNEY MEAD INDUSTRIAL ESTATE
HOLLYWELL BUSINESS CENTRE

6

ROAD
Playing Field

TONYBEE RD
HAW-THORN CL
MAPLE CL
THE GARTH
HILL
RALEIGH PARK RD
SWEETMANS RD

CHESTNUT RD
LABURNUM RD
YARNELLS RD
CEDAR RD
BEECH RD

North Hinksey Village

BY-PASS
A34
NORTH HINKSEY VILLAGE
Schs
Manor Farm
HINKSEY VILLAGE

Bulstake Stream

A B 18 C D

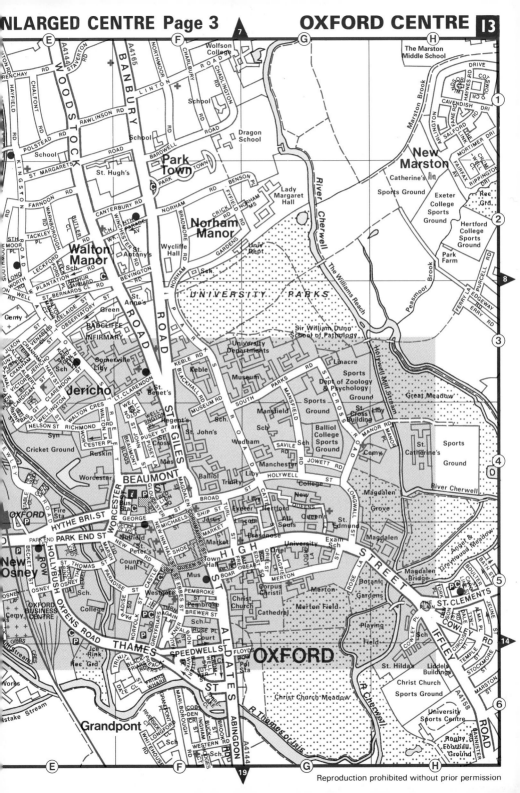

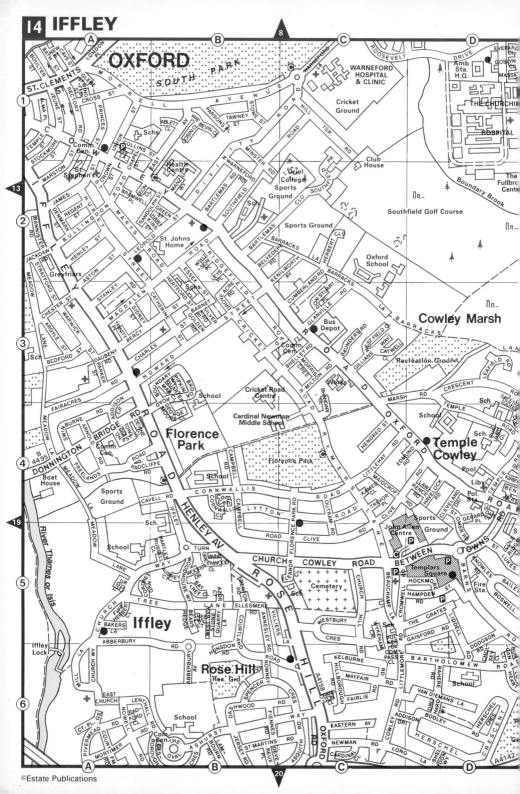

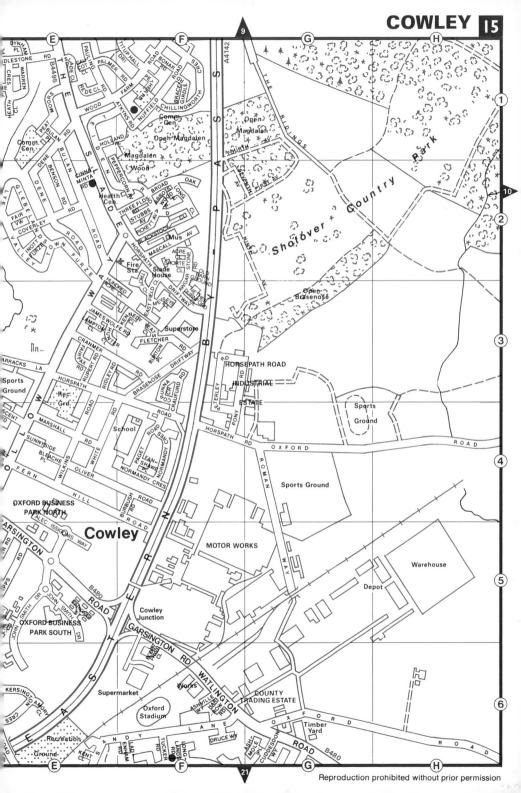

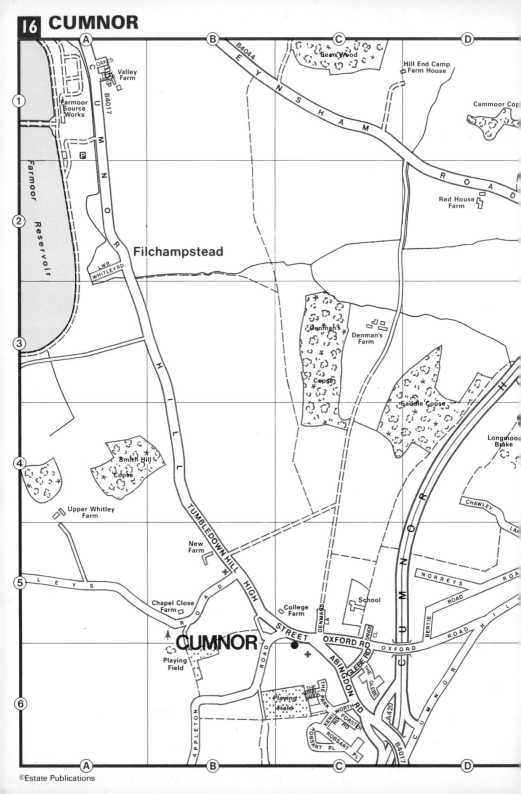

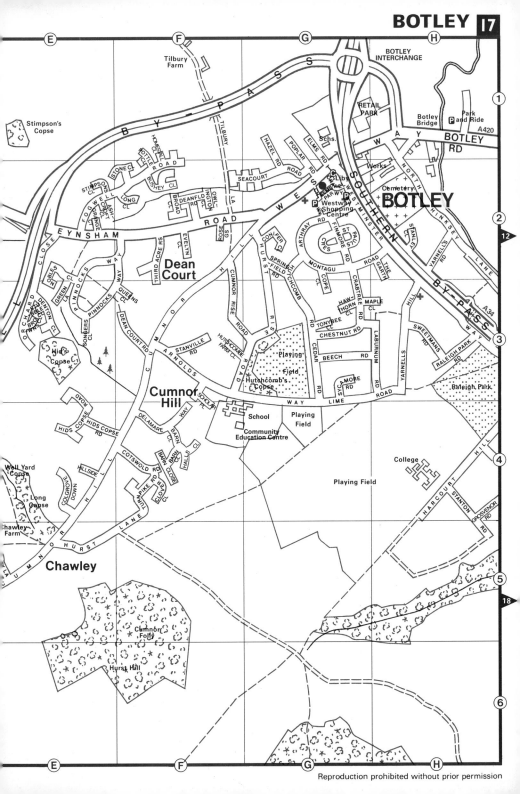

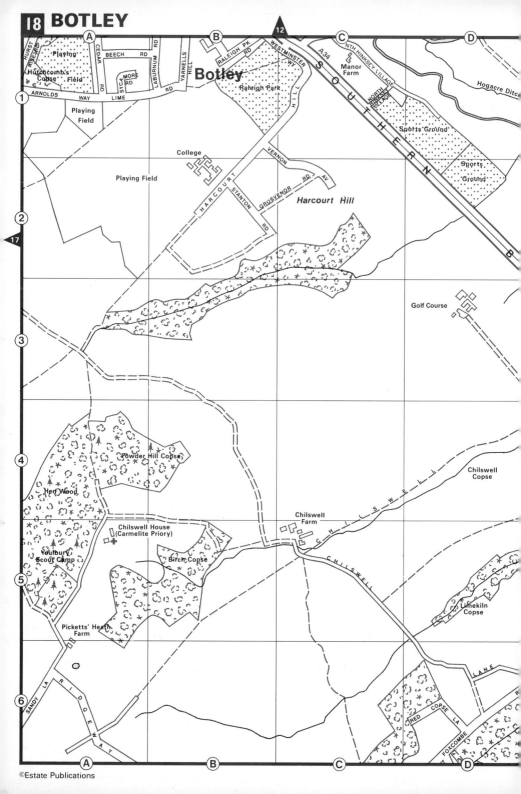

©Estate Publications

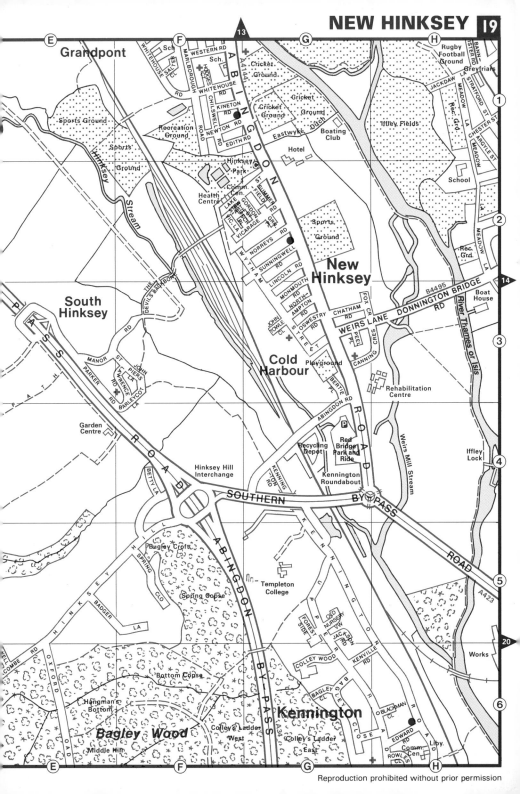

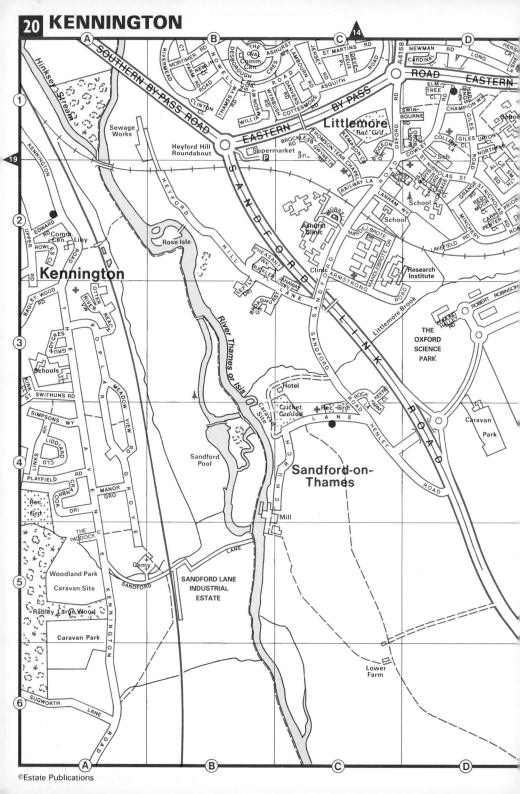

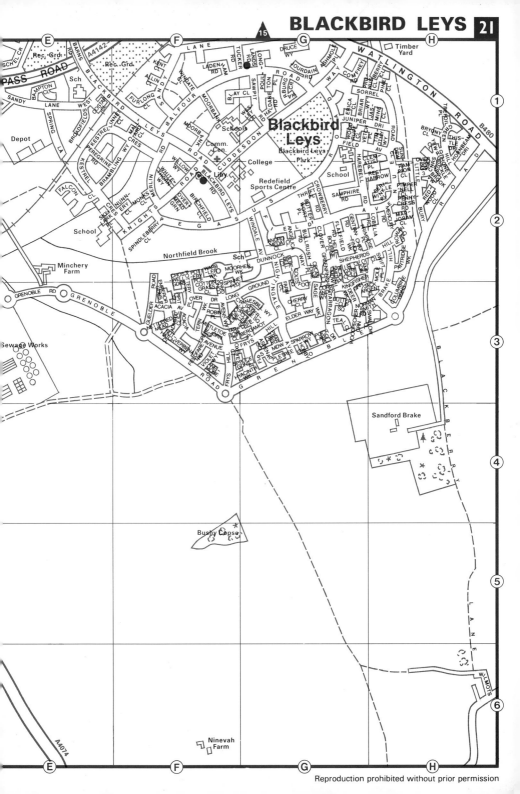

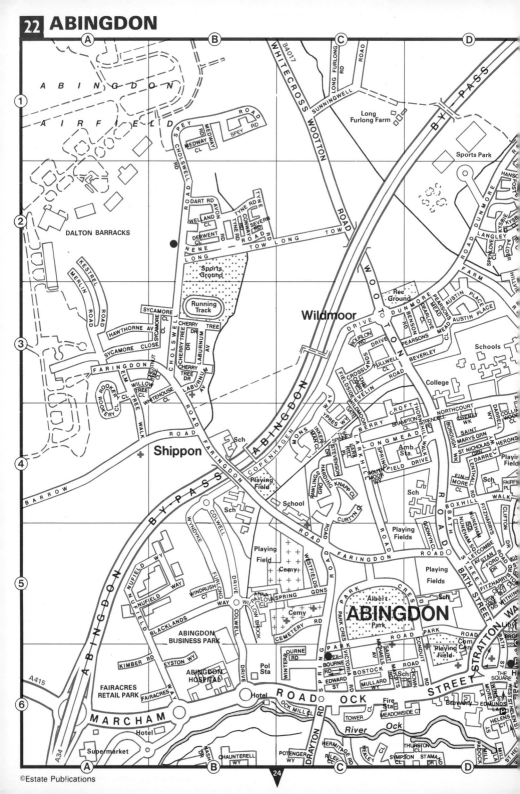

ABINGDON AIRFIELD

DALTON BARRACKS

Sports Park

Long Furlong Farm

Wildmoor

Sports Ground

Running Track

Rec Ground

Schools

College

Shippon

Amb. Sta.

Playing Field

School

Playing Fields

Playing Fields

ABINGDON

Albert Park

ABINGDON BUSINESS PARK

ABINGDON HOSPITAL

FAIRACRES RETAIL PARK

Cemy

Cemy

CEMETERY

Pol Sta

Hotel

MARCHAM

Supermarket

Hotel

Playing Field

Com

Brewery

Fire Sta

TOWER

River Ock

THE SQUARE

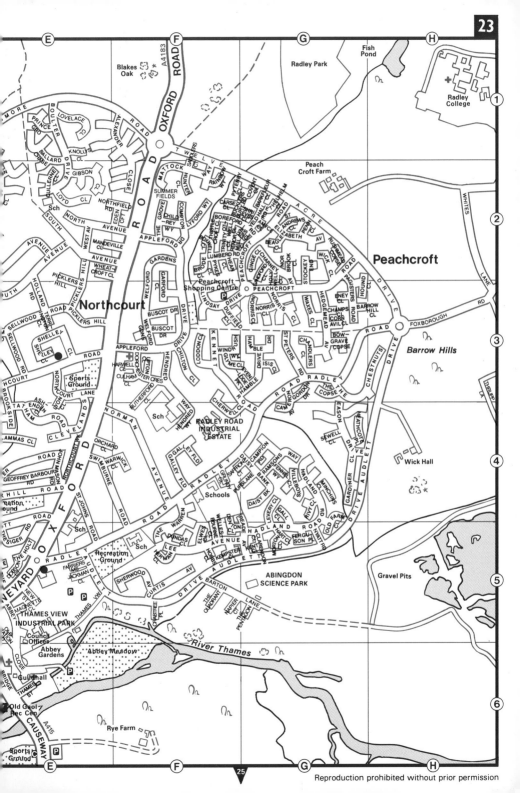

Radley Park

Fish Pond

Blakes Oak

Radley College

Peach Croft Farm

Peachcroft

WHITES LANE

Northcourt

Peachcroft Shopping Centre

PEACHCROFT

Barrow Hills

FOXBOROUGH

CHAMPS CORN AVIL CL

BOW- GRAVE COPSE

THE COPSE

Wick Hall

Sports Ground

RADLEY ROAD INDUSTRIAL ESTATE

Schools

Sch

Gravel Pits

ABINGDON SCIENCE PARK

Recreation Ground

THAMES VIEW INDUSTRIAL PARK

Council Offices

Abbey Gardens

Abbey Meadow

River Thames

Guildhall

Old Gaol Rec Cen

CAUSEWAY

Rye Farm

Sports Ground

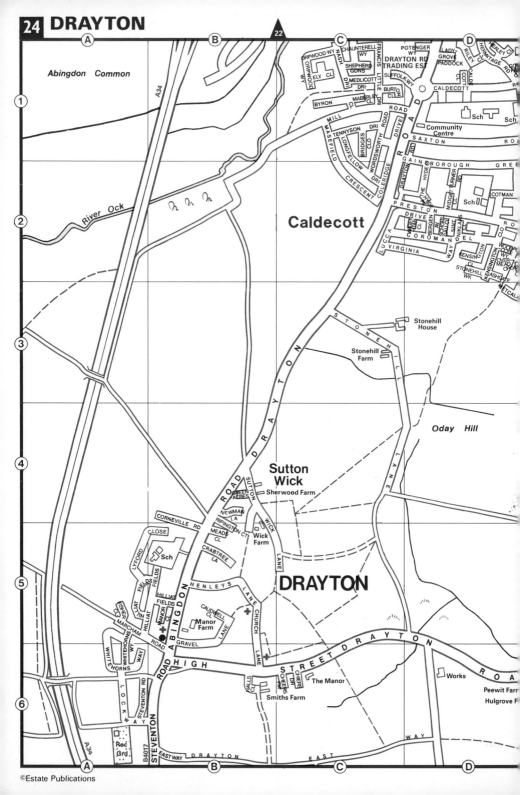

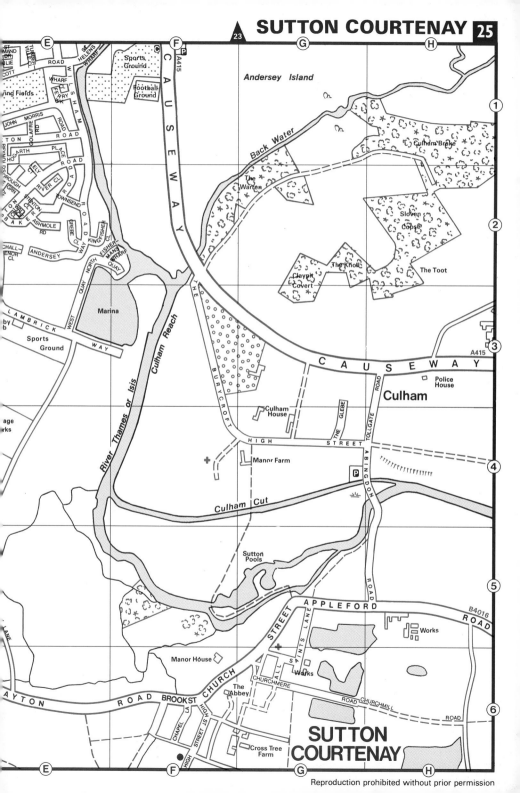

E · C · F · P · A415 · G · H

Sports Ground

Football Ground

Andersey Island

Back Water

Culham Brake

The Warren

Sloven Copse

The Knoll

The Toot

Claypit Covert

1

2

 S WISHAM ROAD · WHARF · FERRY · ST HELENS WHARF

JOHN MORRIS RD · GOLAFRE RD

REVND ALLEN · GARTH · PLACE

PREBOROUGH · ELY · RIVER CI · STANTON · TOWNSEND ROAD

OAK · ASHMOLE RD

CHALL · MENOR CL · ANDERSEY · GREBE RD · KINGFISHER CL · MANS WHARF · NORTH QUAY

WEST QUAY · LAMBRICK WAY

Marina

Sports Ground

age rks

by b

River Thames or Isis

Culham Reach

THE · BURYCROFT

CAUSEWAY · A415

3

C · A · U · S · E · W · A · Y · A415

Police House

**Culham**

Culham House

THE GLEBE ROAD · TOLLGATE ROAD

HIGH STREET

ABINGDON ROAD

Manor Farm

P

4

Culham Cut

Sutton Pools

5

APPLEFORD ROAD

B4016

Works

Manor House

STREET · SAINTS LANE

CHURCH · BROOK ST · CHAPEL LA · HIGH ST · STREET LA · CHURCHMERE

The Abbey

Works

ROAD CHURCHMILL ROAD

6

AYTON · ROAD

Cross Tree Farm

# SUTTON COURTENAY

E · F · HIGH · G · H

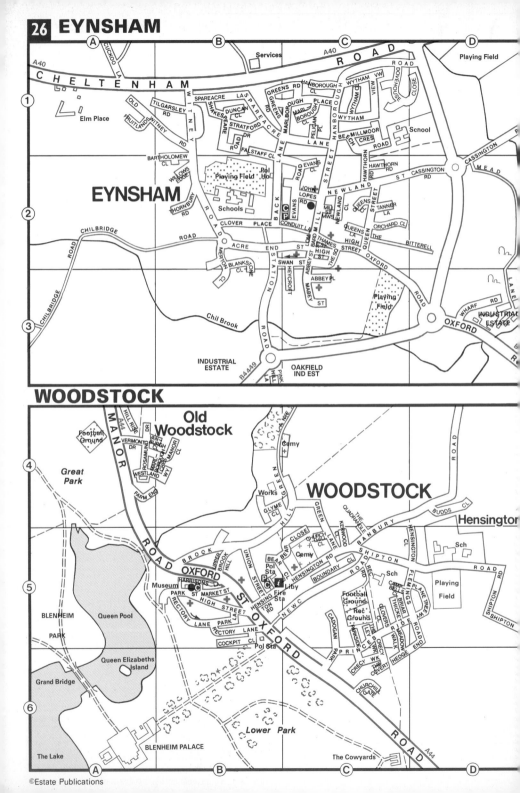

# A - Z  INDEX TO STREETS
## with Postcodes

The Index includes some names for which there is insufficient space on the maps. These names are preceded by an * and are followed by the nearest adjoining thoroughfare.

## OXFORD

Abberbury Av OX4 14 B6
Abberbury Rd. OX4 14 A5
Abbey Rd. OX2 12 D4
Abbots Wood East. OX3 15 F2
Abbots Wood West. OX3 15 F2
Abingdon By-Pass. OX1 19 F5
Abingdon Rd, Cold Harbour. OX1 19 G4
Abingdon Rd. OX2 16 C6
Abingdon Rd, Grandpont. OX1 19 F1
Ablett Clo. OX4 14 B1
Acacia Av. OX4 21 F3
Acland Clo. OX3 8 C6
Acre Clo. OX4 15 F2
Acremead Rd. OX33 10 D4
Addison Cres. OX4 14 A4
Addison Dri. OX4 14 C6
Adelaide St. OX2 13 E3
Admiral Clo. OX4 21 F3
Albert St, Jericho. OX2 3 A1
Albert St. OX1 3 C4
Albion Pl. OX1 3 C4
Aldebarton Rd. OX3 9 E3
Alden Cres. OX3 9 F3
Aldrich Rd. OX2 7 E3
Alec Issigonis Way. OX3 15 E4
Alesworth Grn. OX3 8 C2
Alexandra Rd. OX2 12 D5
Alfred St. OX1 3 D3
Alice Smith Sq. OX4 20 D2
All Saints Rd. OX3 8 D5
Allam St. OX2 3 A1
Allin Clo. OX4 21 F1
Alma Pl. OX4 13 H5
Ambleside Dri. OX3 8 C3
Ambrose Rise. OX33 11 G4
Amory Clo. OX4 15 E6
Andromeda Clo. OX4 21 G2
Anemone Clo. OX4 21 F3
Angelica Clo. OX4 21 G2
Anne Greenwood Clo. OX4 14 B5
Annesley Rd. OX4 14 B5
Anson Clo. OX33 11 G4
Appleton Rd. OX2 16 B6
Appletree Clo. OX4 21 G3
Apsley Rd. OX2 6 D3
Argyle St. OX4 14 A3
Aristotle La. OX4 12 D2
Arlington Dri. OX3 8 A2
Armstrong Rd. OX4 20 D2
Arnold Rd. OX4 14 A4
Arnolds Way. OX2 17 F3
Arthray Rd. OX2 17 G2
Arthur Garrard Clo. OX2 13 E3
Arthur St. OX2 12 D5
Ash Grove. OX3 9 E3
Ashcroft Clo. OX2 17 E2
Ashlong Rd. OX3 8 B2
Ashmore Pl. OX4 21 G1
Ashurst Way. OX4 14 B6
Ashville Way. OX4 15 F6
Aspen Sq. OX4 21 G3
Asquith Rd. OX4 20 C1
Aston St. OX4 14 A2
Atkinson Clo. OX3 9 E2
Atkyns Rd. OX3 15 F1
Atwell Pl. OX3 9 E6
Aubrey Clo. OX4 14 B5
Avens Way. OX4 21 F3
Avenue La. OX4 14 A1
Awgar Stone Rd. OX3 15 F3
Azor Ct. OX4 14 B5

Back La. OX3 7 H6
Badger La. OX1 19 E5
Bagley Clo. OX1 19 G6
Bagley Wood Rd. OX1 20 A3
Bailey Rd. OX4 14 D5
Bainton Rd. OX2 6 D6
Baker Clo. OX3 9 G5
Bakers La. OX4 14 A5
Balfour Rd. OX4 21 F1
Bampton Clo. OX4 21 E1
Banbury Rd. OX2 3 C1
Banbury Rd, Cutteslow. OX2 6 D1
Bankside. OX3 9 F4
Bannister Clo. OX4 14 A2
Bardwell Rd. OX2 7 F6
Barleycott La. OX1 19 F3
Barlow Clo. OX33 11 E4
Barn Clo. OX2 17 F4
Barnet St. OX4 14 B3
Barns Hay. OX3 7 H5
Barns Rd. OX4 14 D5
Barracks La. OX4 14 C3
Barrett St. OX2 13 E5
Barrington Clo. OX3 8 D5
Bartholomew Rd. OX4 14 D6
Bartlemas Clo. OX4 14 B2
Bartlemas Rd. OX4 14 B2
Barton La. OX3 8 D3
Barton Rd. OX3 9 E3
Barton Village Rd. OX3 9 E2
Bassett Rd. OX3 9 F3
Bateman St. OX3 8 D5
Bath St. OX4 14 A6
Bay Tree Clo. OX4 14 B5
Bayswater Farm Rd. OX3 9 G3
Bayswater Rd. OX3 9 F4
Bear La. OX1 3 D3
Bears Hedge. OX4 14 B5
Beauchamp La. OX4 14 C5
Beaumont Bldgs. OX1 3 B2
Beaumont Rd. OX3 9 F5
Beaumont St. OX1 3 B2
Becket St. OX1 3 A3
Bedford St. OX4 14 A3
Beech Rd, Botley. OX2 17 G3
Beech Rd, Headington. OX3 8 D4
Beech Rd, Wheatley. OX33 11 F5
Beechcroft Rd. OX2 7 E5
Beechey Av. OX3 8 A3
Beef La. OX1 3 C4
Belbroughton Rd. OX2 7 E6
Belvedere Rd. OX4 14 B2
Bennett Cres. OX4 14 D4
Benson Pl. OX2 13 F2
Benson Rd. OX3 15 E2
Bergamot Pl. OX4 21 G3
Bernwood Rd. OX3 9 E3
Bertie Pl. OX1 19 G3
Bertie Rd. OX2 16 D5
Betty La. OX1 19 F4
Between Towns Rd. OX4 14 D4
Bevington Rd. OX2 13 F2
Bhandari Clo. OX4 14 C5
Bickerton Rd. OX3 8 D5
Binsey La. OX2 12 B2
Binswood Av. OX3 9 E5
Birchfield Clo. OX4 21 G1
Biscoe Ct. OX33 11 G4
Bishop Kirk Pl. OX2 6 D4
Blackberry La. OX4 21 H3
Blackbird Leys Rd. OX4 21 E1
Blackfriars Rd. OX1 3 B4
Blackhall Rd. OX1 3 C1
Blackman Clo. OX1 19 H6
Blacksmiths Mdw. OX4 21 G2
Blackstock Clo. OX3 15 F2
Blackthorn Clo. OX3 9 E3
Bladon Clo. OX2 6 C3
Blandford Av. OX2 6 C3
Blay Clo. OX4 21 F1
Bleache Pl. OX4 14 D5
Blenheim Dri. OX2 6 C3
Blenheim La. OX33 11 E4
Blenheim Pl. OX4 10 B5

Blenheim Way. OX33 10 A5
Blomfield Pl. OX2 3 A1
Bluebell Ct. OX4 21 G2
Blue Boar St. OX1 3 D3
Bobby Fryer Clo. OX4 15 F6
Bodley Pl. OX2 7 E2
Bodley Rd. OX4 14 D6
Bonar Rd. OX3 9 F6
Bonn Sq. OX1 3 C3
Borrowmead Rd. OX3 8 C2
Boswell Rd. OX4 14 D5
Botley Rd. OX2 12 B5
Boulter St. OX4 14 A6
Boults Clo. OX3 8 A2
Boults La. OX3 8 A2
Boundary Brook Rd. OX4 14 B3
Bourne Clo. OX2 7 E2
Bowness Av. OX3 8 B3
Bracegirdle Rd. OX3 15 F1
Bradmore Rd. OX2 13 F2
Brake Hill. OX4 21 H3
Brambling Way. OX4 21 E2
Brampton Rd. OX3 9 F3
Bramwell Pl. OX4 14 A2
Brasenose Driftway. OX4 15 F3
Brasenose La. OX1 3 D3
Brewer St. OX1 3 C4
Briar Way. OX4 21 G1
Bridge St. OX2 12 D5
Broad Clo. OX2 17 F2
Broad Oak. OX3 15 F2
Broad St. OX1 3 C2
Broad Walk. OX1 3 D4
Broadfields. OX4 21 E1
Broadhead Pl. OX3 8 C2
Broadhurst Gdns. OX4 20 B3
Brocklesby Rd. OX4 20 C1
Brome St. OX3 9 F3
Brook St. OX1 13 F6
Brook Vw. OX4 21 H2
Brookfield Cres. OX3 8 B2
Brooklime Walk. OX4 21 F3
Brookside. OX3 8 C5
Broughton Clo. OX3 8 A2
Browns Clo. OX2 17 E3
Bryony Clo. OX4 21 H1
Buckingham St. OX1 13 F6
Buckler Pl. OX4 20 B2
Buckler Rd. OX2 7 E3
Bulan Pl. OX3 15 E1
Bulan Rd. OX3 15 E1
Bullingdon Rd. OX4 14 A2
Bullrush Rd. OX4 21 G2
Bulstake Clo. OX2 12 C5
Burbush Rd. OX4 15 F4
Burchester Av. OX3 9 F3
Burdell Av. OX3 9 H3
Burgan Clo. OX4 14 D6
Burlington Cres. OX3 9 G4
Burrows Clo. OX3 9 E4
Bursill Clo. OX3 9 H4
Burton Pl. OX4 15 F3
Bushey Clo. OX4 17 F2
Bushey Leys Clo. OX3 9 F3
Butler Clo. OX2 6 C3
Butler Rd. OX2 13 E2
Buttercup Sq. OX4 21 G3
Butterwort Pl. OX4 21 G2
Butterwyke Pl. OX1 3 C4
Butts La. OX3 7 H5
Butts Rd. OX33 10 B6

Calcot Clo. OX3 9 E6
Cambridge Ter. OX1 3 C4
Campbell Rd. OX4 14 B4
Campion Clo. OX4 21 G2
Canal St. OX2 3 A1
Canning Cres. OX4 19 G3
Cannons Field. OX3 8 A1
Canterbury Rd. OX2 13 E2
Capel Clo. OX2 6 D3
Cardigan St. OX2 3 A1
Cardinal Clo. OX4 20 D1
Cardwell Cres. OX3 8 C5
Carey Clo. OX2 6 C2
Carlton Rd. OX2 6 D2

Caroline St. OX4 13 H5
Carpenter Clo. OX4 20 D2
Carters Clo. OX3 9 G5
Castle St. OX1 3 B4
Catherine St. OX4 14 B3
Catte St. OX1 3 D2
Catwell Clo. OX4 14 C3
Cave St. OX4 14 A1
Cavell Rd. OX4 14 B4
Cavendish Dri. OX3 7 H6
Cavendish Rd. OX2 7 E2
Cecil Sharp Pl. OX3 8 D5
Cedar Ct. OX4 14 D4
Cedar Rd. OX2 17 G3
*Centre Rise, Gidley Way. OX33 10 B6
Chadlington Rd. OX2 7 F6
Chaffinch Wk. OX4 21 G2
Champion Way. OX4 20 D1
Chapel La. OX4 20 C2
Chapel St. OX4 14 A1
Chapel Way. OX2 17 G2
Charlbury Rd. OX2 7 F6
Charles St. OX4 14 A3
Chatham Rd. OX1 19 G3
Chawley La. OX2 16 D4
Cheney La. OX3 8 B6
Chequers Pl. OX3 9 F5
Cherry Clo. OX4 21 G3
Cherwell Dri. OX3 8 A2
Cherwell St. OX4 8 A6
Chester St. OX4 14 A3
Chestnut Av. OX3 9 E3
Chestnut Rd. OX2 17 G3
Chillingworth Cres. OX3 15 F1
Chilswell La. OX1 18 C5
Chilswell Path. OX1 18 C5
Chilswell Rd. OX1 19 F1
Chiswell La. OX1 19 E6
Cholsey Clo. OX4 14 D6
Cholesbury Grange. OX3 8 B3
Choswell Gdns. OX4 21 F2
Church Cowley Rd. OX4 14 B5
Church Hill Rd. OX4 14 C5
Church La. OX3 7 H5
Church La. OX4 20 C4
Church Rd, Horspath. OX33 10 A6
Church Rd, Wheatley. OX33 11 E4
Church Walk. OX2 13 E2
Church Way. OX4 14 A5
Churchill Pl. OX2 6 C3
Churchill Dri. OX3 8 D6
Cinnamenta Rd. OX3 15 E2
Circus St. OX4 13 H6
Claymond Rd. OX3 9 G3
Clays Clo. OX3 8 B2
Cleavers Sq. OX4 21 G3
Clematis Pl. OX4 21 H1
Cleveland Dri. OX4 14 D4
Clifford Pl. OX2 6 A3
Clinton Clo. OX4 20 B1
Clive Rd. OX4 14 C4
Clover Clo. OX4 17 F4
Clover Pl. OX4 21 G2
Cobden Cres. OX1 13 F6
Colemans Hill. OX3 9 F4
Coleridge Clo. OX4 14 D5
Collcutt Clo. OX33 10 B6
College Clo. OX33 11 G4
College La. OX4 20 D1
College Way. OX33 10 A6
Colley Wood. OX1 19 G6
Collins St. OX4 14 A1
Collinwood Clo. OX3 9 G4
Collinwood Rd. OX3 9 G4
Colterne Clo. OX3 8 B3
Coltsfoot Sq. OX4 21 G2
Columbine Gdns. OX4 21 H3
Colwell Dri. OX3 9 G3
Combe Rd. OX2 3 A1
Comfrey Rd. OX4 21 G1
Compass Clo. OX4 14 C6
Conifer Clo. OX2 17 G2

Coniston Av. OX3 8 B3
Coolidge Clo. OX3 8 D6
Cooper Pl. OX3 9 F4
Coopers Clo. OX33 10 D4
Cope Clo. OX2 17 G2
Coppock Clo. OX3 9 F5
Copse La. OX3 8 B3
Cordrey Grn. OX4 14 A5
Cornmarket St. OX1 3 C3
Cornwallis Clo. OX4 14 B4
Cornwallis Rd. OX4 14 B4
Corriander Way. OX4 21 G3
Corunna Cres. OX4 15 F3
Cosin Clo. OX4 14 B1
Costar Clo. OX4 21 E1
Cotswold Cres. OX3 8 A2
Cotswold Rd. OX2 17 F4
Cottesmore Rd. OX4 20 C1
Cotton Grass Clo. OX4 21 F3
Court Farm Rd. OX4 14 A6
Court Pl Gdns. OX4 14 A6
Courtland Rd. OX4 14 B5
Coverley Rd. OX3 15 E2
Cowley Pl. OX4 3 F4
Cowley Rd. OX4 14 A1
Cowley Rd, Littlemore. OX4 20 D1
Crabtree Rd. OX4 17 G3
Cranbrook Dri. OX1 20 A4
Cranesbill Way. OX4 21 F3
Cranham St. OX2 3 A1
Cranham Ter. OX2 3 A1
Cranley Rd. OX3 9 G3
Cranmer Rd. OX4 15 E3
Cranston Clo. OX4 14 C6
Craufurd Rd. OX4 15 F3
Crescent Clo. OX4 14 D3
Crescent Rd. OX4 14 D3
Cress Hill Pl. OX3 9 F3
Crick Rd. OX2 13 F2
Cricket Rd. OX4 14 B3
Cripley Pl. OX2 12 D4
Cripley Rd. OX2 13 E4
Croft Clo. OX3 8 A3
Croft Rd. OX3 8 A3
Cromwell Clo. OX3 8 A3
Cromwell Rd. OX4 14 C5
Cromwell St. OX1 3 C4
Cross St. OX4 14 A1
Crotch Cres. OX3 8 B3
Crowberry Rd. OX4 21 G2
Crown Rd. OX33 11 F4
Crown St. OX4 14 A2
Cuckoo La. OX3 8 A5
Cuddesdon Rd. OX33 10 A6
Cuddesdon Way. OX4 21 F2
Cullum Rd. OX33 11 G5
Cumberland Rd. OX4 14 C3
Cumberlege Clo. OX3 7 H4
Cummings Clo. OX3 9 F5
Cumnor Hill, Chawley. OX2 16 D6
Cumnor Hill, Filchampstead. OX2 16 A1
Cumnor Hill By-Pass. OX2 16 D6
Cumnor Rise Rd. OX2 17 F3
Cunliffe Clo. OX2 7 E5
Curl Clo. OX3 9 E3
Cyprus Ter. OX2 6 C3

Dale Clo. OX1 13 F6
Danvers Rd. OX4 20 C1
Dashwood Rd. OX4 14 B6
Daubeny Rd. OX4 14 A3
Davenant Rd. OX2 6 C3
David Nichols Clo. OX4 20 C2
David Walter Clo. OX2 7 E2
Dawson Pl. OX2 13 E4
Dawson St, Jericho. OX2 3 A1
Dawson St. OX4 13 H5
Dead Mans Walk. OX1 3 D4
Dean Court Rd. OX2 17 F3
Deanfield Rd. OX2 17 F2
Deer Wk. OX4 21 G3
Delbush Av. OX3 9 H3
Dene Rd. OX3 15 E2
Denmans La. OX2 16 C5

Denmark St. OX4 14 A2
Denton Clo. OX2 17 E3
Dents Clo. OX3 8 B2
Derwent Av. OX3 8 B3
Desborough Cres. OX4 20 B1
Desmesne Furze. OX3 8 C6
Devereux Pl. OX4 20 C1
Devine Clo. OX4 14 A4
Diamond Pl. OX2 7 E5
Divinity Rd. OX4 14 B2
Dodgson Rd. OX4 14 D5
Don Boscoe Clo. OX4 14 D4
Don Stuart Pl. OX4 14 C3
Donnington Bridge Rd. OX4 14 A4
Dorchester Clo. OX3 9 F6
Doris Field Clo. OX3 8 B4
Dove House Clo. OX2 6 C3
Downside End. OX3 9 G4
Downside Rd. OX3 9 G5
Doyley Rd. OX2 12 D5
Drove Acre Rd. OX4 14 B3
Druce Way. OX4 15 F6
Dudgeon Dri. OX4 20 C1
Duke St. OX2 12 C5
Dunnock Way. OX4 21 G2
Dunstan Rd. OX3 8 C3
Dynham Pl. OX3 9 E6

Earl St. OX2 12 C5
East Av. OX4 14 B1
East Church. OX4 14 A6
East Field Clo. OX3 15 F3
East St. OX2 12 D5
Eastern Av. OX4 14 C6
Eastern By-Pass. OX3 9 F4
Eastern By-Pass Rd. OX4 20 B1
Eden Dri. OX3 8 B3
Edgecombe Rd. OX3 9 F3
Edgeway Rd. OX3 8 A4
Edith Rd. OX1 19 F1
Edmund Halley Rd. OX4 20 D3
Edmund Rd. OX4 14 D4
Edward Rd. OX1 19 H6
Egerton Rd. OX4 14 B5
Elder Way. OX4 21 G3
Eleanor Clo. OX4 14 C5
Ellesmere Rd. OX4 14 B5
Elm Clo. OX33 11 G5
Elm Tree Clo. OX4 20 D1
Elms Dri. OX3 8 A2
Elms Par. OX2 17 G2
Elms Rd. OX2 17 G1
Elmthorpe Rd. OX2 6 B3
Elsfield Rd. OX3 8 A1
Elsfield Way. OX2 7 E2
Emperor Gdns. OX4 21 F3
Elton Cres. OX33 11 G5
Erica Clo. OX4 21 G1
Essex St. OX4 14 B2
Ethelred Ct. OX3 8 D3
Evelyn Clo. OX2 17 F2
Everard Clo. OX3 8 D6
Ewert Pl. OX2 7 E5
Ewin Clo. OX3 8 A2
Eynsham Rd. OX2 16 B1

Faber Clo. OX4 20 D2
Fair View. OX3 15 E2
Fairacres Rd. OX4 14 A4
Fairfax Gate. OX33 11 F4
Fairfax Rd. OX4 15 E3
Fairlawn End. OX2 6 C3
Fairlie Rd. OX4 14 C6
Falcon Clo. OX4 21 E2
Fane Rd. OX3 7 H6
Fanshawe Pl. OX4 15 F4
Farm Clo. OX4 21 G2
Farm Close La. OX33 11 F4
Farm Close Rd. OX33 11 F4
Farmer Pl. OX3 8 A3
Farmoor Ct. OX2 16 A1
Farndon Rd. OX2 13 E2
Faulkner St. OX1 3 C4
Feilden Gro. OX3 8 B4
Fern Hill Rd. OX4 15 E4
Ferry Hinksey Rd. OX2 12 D6
Ferry La. OX3 13 H3
Ferry Pool Rd. OX2 7 E5
Ferry Rd. OX3 8 A4
Fettiplace Rd. OX3 9 E2
Field Av. OX4 21 G1
Field House Dri. OX4 6 D3
Fieldfare Rd. OX4 21 F3

Fiennes Rd. OX4 14 B6
Finch Clo. OX3 8 C6
Finmore Rd. OX2 17 G2
Firs Mdw. OX4 21 G3
First Av. OX3 15 G2
First Turn. OX2 6 C3
Fitzherbert Clo. OX4 14 A5
Five Mile Dri. OX2 6 C2
Flaxfield Rd. OX4 21 G2
Fletcher Rd. OX4 15 F3
Flexney Pl. OX3 9 E6
Florence Park Rd. OX4 14 C5
Floyds Row. OX1 3 D4
Fogwell Rd. OX2 17 E2
Fords Clo. OX33 10 A6
Forest Rd. OX3 9 F4
Forest Side. OX1 19 G5
Forster Rd. OX2 16 C6
Fortnam Clo. OX3 8 C4
Fourth Av. OX3 15 F1
Fox Cres. OX1 19 G3
Foxcombe Rd. OX1 18 D6
Foxton Clo. OX2 6 C2
Foxwell Dri. OX3 8 C2
Franklin Rd. OX3 8 C4
Freelands Rd. OX4 14 A4
Frenchay Rd. OX2 6 D6
Frewin Ct. OX1 3 C3
Friars Wharf. OX1 13 F6
Friday La. OX33 11 F4
Frieze Way. OX 5 G6
Frys Hill. OX4 21 F3
Furlong Clo. OX4 21 F1
Fyfield Rd. OX2 13 F2

Gaisford Rd. OX4 14 D5
Gardiner Clo. OX33 11 F4
Gardiner St. OX3 8 D5
Garford Rd. OX2 7 F6
Garsington Rd. OX4 15 E5
Gateley. OX33 10 B6
Gathorne Rd. OX3 9 E5
Gentian Rd. OX4 21 G2
George Moore Clo. OX4 14 B4
George St. OX1 3 B3
George Street Mews. OX1 3 B3
Gerard Pl. OX4 14 D4
Gibbs Cres. OX2 3 A4
Gidley Way. OX33 10 B6
Giles Clo. OX4 20 D1
Giles Rd. OX4 20 D1
Gillians Way. OX4 14 C3
Gipsy La. OX3 8 C5
Girdlestone Clo. OX3 9 E6
Girdlestone Rd. OX3 8 D6
Gladstone Rd. OX3 9 E4
Glanville Rd. OX4 14 C3
Glebe St. OX4 14 A1
Glebelands. OX3 15 E2
Gloucester La. OX1 3 B2
Gloucester St. OX1 3 C2
Godstow Rd. OX2 6 A4
Golden Rd. OX4 14 B3
Goose Green Clo. OX2 6 B3
Gordon Clo. OX3 8 A2
Gordon St. OX1 19 G2
Gorse Leas. OX3 8 C2
Goslyn Clo. OX3 8 D6
Gouldland Gdns. OX3 8 C2
Grandpont Pl. OX1 13 F6
Grange Ct. OX2 17 E2
Grange Rd. OX4 20 D2
Granville Ct. OX3 8 B6
Grays Rd. OX3 8 C5
Great Clarendon St. OX2 3 A1
Great Mead. OX1 3 A2
Grebe Clo. OX4 21 F3
Green Hill. OX4 21 H1
Green La. OX2 17 E3
Green Pl. OX1 19 G2
Green Ridge. OX3 9 G3
Green Rd. OX3 9 F4
Green St. OX4 14 B2
Greenfinch Clo. OX4 21 G3
Grenoble Rd. OX4S 21 E3
Grosvenor Rd. OX2 18 B2
Grove St. OX3 6 D4
Grovelands Rd. OX3 9 G5
Grundy Cres. OX1 20 A3
Grunsell Clo. OX3 8 C2
Guelder Rd. OX4 21 G3
Gurden Pl. OX3 9 F3

Gwyneth Rd. OX4 20 C1

Hadow Rd. OX3 8 B3
Haldane Rd. OX4 21 G1
Hall St. OX1 1 C3
Halliday Hill. OX3 8 C2
Hamilton Rd. OX2 7 E4
Hampden Rd. OX4 14 D5
Handfield Pl. OX3 9 F3
Harberton Mead. OX3 8 A4
Harbord Rd. OX2 6 D2
Harcourt Hill. OX2 18 B2
Harcourt Ter. OX3 8 C5
Hardings Clo. OX4 20 D1
Harebell Rd. OX4 21 G1
Harefields. OX2 6 D2
Harley Rd. OX2 12 C5
Harold White Clo. OX3 9 G5
Harolde Clo. OX3 9 E3
Harpes Rd. OX2 7 E3
Harrow Rd. OX4 15 F6
Hart St. OX2 3 A1
Hartley Russell Clo. OX4 14 B5
Haslemere Gdns. OX2 7 E4
Hathaways. OX33 11 F4
Havelock Rd. OX4 14 D4
Hawkins St. OX4 14 B2
Hawksmoor Rd. OX2 6 D2
Hawkswell Gdns. OX2 7 E4
Hawthorn Av. OX3 9 E4
Hawthorn Clo. OX2 17 G3
Hayes Clo. OX3 8 A4
Hayfield Rd. OX2 6 D6
Haynes Rd. OX3 7 H6
Hayward Rd. OX2 6 D1
Hazel Rd. OX2 17 G1
Headington Rd. OX3 8 A6
Headley Way. OX3 8 B3
Heath Clo. OX3 15 E1
Heather Pl. OX3 8 A1
Hedges Clo. OX3 9 F4
Helen Rd. OX2 12 D5
Hellebourine Clo. OX4 21 G2
Hendred St. OX4 14 C4
Hengrove Clo. OX3 9 E3
Henley Av. OX4 14 B4
Henley Rd. OX4 20 C4
Henley St. OX4 14 A2
Henry Rd. OX2 12 D5
Henry Taunt Clo. OX3 9 F3
Herbert Clo. OX4 14 C2
Hernes Clo. OX2 7 E3
Hernes Rd. OX2 7 E3
Hernes Rd Cres. OX2 7 E3
Heron Pl. OX4 7 E3
Herschel Cres. OX4 14 B6
Hertford St. OX4 14 B3
Heyford Hill La. OX4 20 B2
Hids Copse Rd. OX2 17 E4
High Cross Way. OX3 9 F3
High St. OX2 16 B5
High St. OX1 3 D3
High St. OX3 11 E4
Highfield Av. OX3 8 D6
*Hill Rise,
 Gidley Way. OX33 10 B6
Hill Top Rd. OX4 14 C1
Hill View. OX3 9 H3
Hill View Rd. OX2 12 D5
Hillary Way. OX33 11 G5
Hillborough Rd. OX4 14 C6
Hillside. OX2 17 E4
Hinksey Hill. OX1 19 E5
Hobby Ct. OX4 21 G3
Hobson Rd. OX2 6 D4
Hockmore St. OX4 14 D5
Hodges Ct. OX1 19 F1
Holland Pl. OX3 15 E1
Holley Cres. OX3 9 E5
Hollow Way. OX4 14 D4
Holloway Rd. OX33 11 F4
Hollybush Row. OX1 3 A3
Holt Weer Clo. OX2 7 E2
Holyoake Rd. OX3 9 E4
Holywell St. OX1 3 D2
Home Clo. OX2 6 A3
Homestall Clo. OX2 17 F1
Honeysuckle Gro. OX4 21 H2
Hornbeam Dri. OX4 21 H1
Horseman Clo. OX3 8 A2
Horspath Driftway. OX3 15 F2
Horspath Rd. OX4 15 E3
Horwood Clo. OX3 8 D5
Hosker Clo. OX3 9 G4

Howard St. OX4 14 A3
Howe Clo. OX33 11 F4
Hugh Allen Cres. OX3 8 A4
Humfrey Rd. OX3 9 G3
Hundred Acres Clo. OX3 15 E2
Hunsdon Rd. OX4 14 B6
Hunter Clo. OX4 15 E3
Hurst La. OX2 17 E5
Hurst Rise Rd. OX2 17 G2
Hurst St. OX4 14 A2
Hutchcomb Rd. OX2 17 G2
Hutchcombe Farm Clo. OX2 17 F3
Hyacinth Walk. OX4 21 F3
Hythe Bridge St. OX1 3 A3

Iffley Rd. OX4 3 F4
Iffley Turn. OX4 14 B4
Islip Rd. OX3 9 F3

INDUSTRIAL & RETAIL:
County Trading Est. OX4 15 G6
Horspath Rd Ind Est. OX4 15 G3
Littleworth Business Centre. OX33 10 D5
Osney Mead Ind Est. OX2 12 D6
Oxford Business Pk. OX2 6 D1
Oxford Business Pk Nth. OX4 15 E4
Oxford Business Pk Sth. OX4 15 E5
Sandford La Ind Est. OX4 20 B5
The Oxford Science Pk. OX4 20 D3

Ingle Clo. OX3 8 C3
Inott Furze. OX3 15 E2
Ivy La. OX2 8 D3

Jack Argent Clo. OX4 21 G3
Jack Straws La. OX3 8 A4
Jackdaw La. OX4 14 A2
Jackies La. OX33 11 G5
Jackson La. OX1 19 G5
Jackson Rd. OX2 7 E2
James St. OX4 14 A2
James Wolfe Rd. OX4 15 E3
Janaway Pl. OX4 20 C2
Jasmine Clo. OX4 21 H1
Jericho St. OX2 3 A1
Jersey Rd. OX4 14 B6
Jessops Clo. OX3 8 C2
Jeune St. OX4 13 H5
John Buchan Rd. OX3 8 C2
John Garne Way. OX3 8 A5
John Piers La. OX1 19 F3
John Smith Dri. OX4 15 E5
John Snow Pl. OX3 9 F4
John Towle Clo. OX1 19 G3
Jordan Hill. OX2 6 D1
Jourdains Rd. OX4 21 G1
Jowett Walk. OX1 3 E2
Junction Rd. OX4 14 D4
Juniper Dri. OX4 21 G1
Juxon St. OX2 3 A1

Kames Clo. OX4 14 C4
Keble Rd. OX1 3 C1
Keene Clo. OX4 20 C3
Kelburne Rd. OX4 14 C6
Kelham Hall Dri. OX33 11 F5
Kellys Rd. OX33 10 D4
Kempson Cres. OX4 20 C1
Kendall Cres. OX2 7 E2
Kenilworth Av. OX4 14 B2
Kenilworth Rd. OX2 16 C6
Kennedy Clo. OX4 15 F3
Kennett Rd. OX3 8 D5
Kennington Rd. OX1 19 G4
Kent Clo. OX4 21 F1
Kenville Rd. OX1 19 G6
Kersington Cres. OX4 15 E6
Kestrel Cres. OX4 21 F3
Keydale Rd. OX33 10 D4
Kiln La. OX3 9 G5
Kiln La. OX33 11 G4
Kimber Clo. OX33 11 F4
Kineton Rd. OX1 19 F1
King Edward St. OX1 3 D3
King St. OX2 3 A1
Kingfisher Grn. OX4 21 G3

Kings Cross Rd. OX2 7 E3
Kings Mill La. OX3 8 A6
Kingston Rd. OX2 13 E2
Kirby Pl. OX4 14 D4
Kirk Clo. OX2 6 D2
Kirk Clo. OX1 20 A3
Knights Rd. OX4 21 F2
Knightshouse. OX3 9 G6
Knolles Rd. OX4 14 D8
Kybald St. OX1 3 D3

Laburnum Rd. OX2 17 H3
Ladder Hill. OX33 11 E6
Ladenham Rd. OX4 21 F1
Lake St. OX1 19 F2
Lakefield Rd. OX4 20 D2
Lakeside. OX2 6 C1
Lakeside Av. OX2 6 C1
Lamarsh Rd. OX2 12 C5
Lambourn Rd. OX4 20 C1
Lampton Clo. OX4 15 E3
Langley Clo. OX3 9 E6
Lanham Way. OX4 20 C2
Larkfields. OX3 9 E6
Larkins La. OX3 8 D3
Lathbury Rd. OX2 7 E6
Latimer Grange. OX3 8 D6
Latimer Rd. OX3 8 D6
Laurel Farm Clo. OX3 8 D3
Lawrence Rd. OX4 14 D4
Leafield Rd. OX4 14 D5
Leckford Pl. OX2 13 E2
Leckford Rd. OX2 13 E2
Leiden Rd. OX3 15 E1
Lenthall Rd. OX4 14 A6
Leon Clo. OX4 14 A2
Leopold St. OX4 14 A2
Lewell Av. OX3 8 A3
Lewis Clo. OX3 9 G6
Leys Pl. OX4 14 B2
Leys Rd. OX2 16 A2
Leyshon Rd. OX33 11 G6
Liddell Rd. OX4 14 D6
Liddiard Clo. OX1 20 A4
Lime Rd. OX2 17 G3
Lime Walk. OX3 8 D6
Lincoln Rd. OX1 19 G2
Links Rd. OX1 20 A4
Linkside Av. OX2 6 C2
Linnet Clo. OX4 21 E1
Linton Rd. OX2 7 E6
Litford Clo. OX4 20 D2
Little Acreage. OX3 8 A1
Little Brewery St. OX4 8 A6
Little Bury. OX4 21 H2
Little Clarendon St. OX1 3 B1
Littlegate St. OX1 3 C4
Littlehay Rd. OX4 14 C4
Littlemore Rd. OX4 14 C6
Littleworth Rd. OX33 10 D5
Lobelia Rd. OX4 21 H2
Lockheart Cres. OX4 14 D6
Lodge Clo. OX3 7 H4
Logic La. OX1 3 E3
London Pl. OX4 8 A6
London Rd. OX3 8 C5
London Rd. OX33 11 F4
Long Clo. OX3 15 F2
Long Clo. OX2 17 F2
Long Ground. OX4 21 F3
Long La. OX4 20 D1
Longford Clo. OX1 13 F6
Longlands Rd. OX4 21 G1
Longwall St. OX1 3 E2
Longworth Rd. OX2 13 E2
Lonsdale Rd. OX2 7 E4
Lovelace Rd. OX2 6 D2
Lovelace Sq. OX2 6 D2
Lower Fisher Row. OX1 3 B3
Lower Whitley Rd. OX2 16 A2
Lucerne Rd. OX2 7 E3
Luther St. OX1 13 F6
Lydia Clo. OX3 9 F4
Lye Valley. OX3 15 E2
Lyndworth Clo. OX3 9 F4
Lyndworth Mews. OX3 9 F4
Lynn Clo. OX3 8 A4
Lytton Rd. OX4 14 B4

Magdalen Bri. OX1 3 F3
Magdalen Rd. OX4 14 A3
Magdalen St. OX1 3 C2
Magpie La. OX1 3 D3
Maidcroft Rd. OX4 14 C4
Malford Rd. OX3 9 G3
Mallard Clo. OX4 21 F1

Maltfield Rd. OX3 8 B2
Mandlebrote Dri. OX4 20 C2
Manor Dri. OX33 10 B6
Manor Farm Rd. OX33 10 A6
Manor Gro. OX1 20 A4
Manor Pl. OX1 3 F2
Manor Rd. OX1 3 E2
Manor Rd, Sth Hinksey. OX1 19 E3
Mansfield Rd. OX1 3 D1
Manzil Way. OX4 14 B2
Maple Clo. OX2 17 H3
Margaret Rd. OX3 9 E5
Marigold Clo. OX4 21 G2
Marjoram Clo. OX4 21 H2
Mark Rd. OX3 9 E5
Market St. OX1 3 C3
Marlborough Clo. OX4 20 D1
Marlborough Rd. OX1 19 F1
Marriott Clo. OX2 6 D2
Marsh La. OX3 8 B3
Marsh Rd. OX4 14 C3
Marshall Rd. OX4 15 E4
Marston Ferry Rd. OX2 7 E5
Marston Rd. OX3 8 A5
Marston St. OX4 14 A2
Martin Ct. OX2 6 D4
Mascall Av. OX3 15 F2
Masons Rd. OX3 9 F6
Massey Clo. OX3 8 D6
Mather Rd. OX3 9 F3
Mattock Clo. OX3 9 E5
Mayfair Rd. OX2 14 C6
Mayfield Rd. OX2 7 E4
Meadenhill. OX3 8 C2
Meadow La. OX4 14 A2
Meadow Prospect. OX2 6 A3
Meadow Vw Rd. OX1 20 A3
Mercury Rd. OX4 21 H2
Mere Rd. OX4 6 C2
Merewood Av. OX3 9 G3
Merlin Rd. OX4 21 H2
Merrivale Sq. OX2 12 D2
Merton Gro. OX1 3 D3
Merton St. OX1 3 D3
Meyseys Clo. OX3 15 F3
Middle Way. OX2 6 D3
Mileway Gdns. OX3 8 D6
Mill La, Iffley. OX4 14 A6
Mill La, Marston. OX3 7 H3
Mill Rd. OX2 6 A3
Mill St. OX4 3 A4
Millbank. OX4 13 E5
Miller Rd. OX33 11 G5
Millers Acre. OX2 7 E2
Millway Clo. OX2 6 C3
Milne Pl. OX3 6 C3
Milton Rd. OX4 14 C3
Minchery Rd. OX4 20 D2
Minster Rd. OX4 14 B1
Mistletoe Grn. OX4 21 F3
Monks Clo. OX4 14 C3
Monmouth Rd. OX1 19 G3
Mole Pl. OX4 21 H2
Montagu Rd. OX2 17 G2
Moody Rd. OX3 8 A4
Moorbank. OX4 21 F1
Moorhen Walk. OX4 21 F2
Moreton Rd. OX2 7 E5
Morland Clo. OX33 11 F4
Morrell Av. OX4 14 A1
Morrell Cres. OX4 20 C2
Morris Cres. OX4 14 C3
Mortimer Dri. OX3 8 A3
Mortimer Rd. OX4 14 A6
Mount St. OX2 3 A1
Mulberry Clo. OX4 21 H1
Mulberry Dri. OX33 11 F4
Museum Rd. OX1 3 C1

Napier Rd. OX4 15 E5
Nash Ct. OX4 15 E5
Nelson St. OX2 3 A2
Nether Durnford Clo. OX4 15 F3
Netherwoods Rd. OX3 9 G5
Nettlebed Mead. OX4 21 F3
New Castle La. OX1 3 D2
New Cross Rd. OX3 9 F4
New High St. OX3 8 D5
New Inn. OX1 3 C3
New Rd. OX1 3 B3
New St. OX4 8 A6
Newlin Clo. OX4 20 B1
Newman Rd. OX4 20 D1
Newton Rd. OX1 19 F1

Nicholas Av. OX3 8 A3
Nicholson Rd. OX3 8 A4
Nightingale Av. OX4 21 G2
Ninth Av. OX4 15 G2
Nobles Clo. OX4 17 E2
Norfolk St. OX1 3 C4
Norham Gdns. OX2 13 F2
Norham Rd. OX2 13 F2
Normandy Cres. OX4 15 F4
Norman Smith Rd. OX4 21 G3
Norreys Rd. OX2 16 D5
Norreys Rd. OX2 19 G2
North Hinksey La. OX2 17 H2
North Hinksey Village. OX2 12 C6
North Parade Av. OX2 13 F2
North Pl. OX3 8 D4
North St. OX2 12 D5
North Way. OX3 6 C2
North Way. OX3 8 C2
Northampton Rd. OX1 19 G3
Northern By-Pass. OX2 6 A1
Northfield Clo. OX4 20 D1
Northfield Rd. OX3 9 E4
Northmoor Rd. OX2 7 E6
Norton Clo. OX3 8 D5
Nowell Rd. OX4 20 B1
Nuffield Rd. OX3 9 F6
Nunnery Clo. OX4 21 F2
Nursery Clo. OX3 8 D6
Nuthatch Clo. OX4 21 F3
Nye Bevan Clo. OX4 14 B1

Oakes La. OX2
Oakthorpe Pl. OX2 7 E5
Oakthorpe Rd. OX2 7 E5
Oatlands Rd. OX2 12 D5
Observatory St. OX2 13 E3
Old Barn Ground. OX3 15 F2
Old Greyfriars St. OX1 3 C4
Old High St. OX3 8 D4
Old London Rd. OX33 11 G4
Old Marston Rd. OX3 8 A3
Old Nursery Vw. OX1 19 G5
Old Rd. OX33 10 A3
Old Rd. OX3 8 C6
Oliver Rd. OX4 15 E4
Orchard Clo. OX2 17 E3
Orchard Clo. OX33 11 F5
Orchard Way. OX4 14 D6
Oriel Sq. OX1 3 C4
Oriel St. OX1 3 D3
Osberton Rd. OX2 6 D4
Osborne Clo. OX2 6 C3
Osler Rd. OX3 8 D4
Osney La. OX1 3 A4
Osney Mead. OX2 12 D6
Oswestry Rd. OX1 19 G3
Otter Reach. OX1 20 A3
Ouseley Clo. OX3 8 A3
Outram Rd. OX4 14 C4
Overbrook Gdns. OX4 21 H2
Overdale Clo. OX3 9 E3
Overmead Grn. OX4 21 F2
Owlington Clo. OX2 17 F2
Oxeye Ct. OX4 21 F3
Oxford Rd, Blackbird Leys. OX4 15 G6
Oxford Rd, Cowley. OX4 15 G4
Oxford Rd. OX2 16 C5
Oxford Rd. OX33 10 A6
Oxford Rd, Littlemore. OX4 20 C1
Oxford Rd. OX3 7 H5
Oxford Rd, Temple Cowley. OX4 14 C4
Oxpens Rd. OX1 3 A4

Paddox Clo. OX2 6 D3
Paget Rd. OX4 15 F4
Palmer Rd. OX3 9 E6
Paradise Sq. OX1 3 B4
Paradise St. OX1 3 B3
Park Clo. OX2 7 E1
Park End Pl. OX1 3 B3
Park End St. OX1 3 A3
Park Hill. OX33 11 F3
Park Town. OX2 13 F2
Park Way. OX3 7 H4
Parker Rd. OX1 19 E3
Parker St. OX4 14 A3
Parks Rd. OX1 3 C1

Parkway Ct. OX4 15 E5
Parry Clo. OX3 8 A4
Parsons Pl. OX4 14 B1
Partridge Wk. OX4 21 H2
Pauling Rd. OX3 9 E6
Peacock Rd. OX3 8 A4
Peartree Clo. OX4 21 G3
Peat Moors. OX3 15 E1
Peel Pl. OX1 19 G3
*Pegasus Grange, Western Rd. OX1 13 F6
Pegasus Rd. OX4 21 F2
Pembroke Sq. OX1 3 C4
Pembroke St. OX1 3 C4
Pennycress Rd. OX4 21 H2
Pennyfarthing Pl. OX1 3 C4
Pennywell Dri. OX2 7 E2
Peppercorn Av. OX3 15 F2
Percy St. OX4 14 A3
Peregrine Rd. OX4 21 E1
Periwinkle Pl. OX4 21 H2
Perrin St. OX3 8 D5
Peterley Rd. OX4 15 F4
Pether Rd. OX3 15 F1
Pheasant Walk. OX4 20 B2
Phipps Rd. OX4 15 E5
Phoebe Ct. OX2 6 D5
Pickett Av. OX3 15 F2
Pike Ter. OX1 3 C4
Pimpernel Clo. OX4 21 H2
Pine Clo. OX4 21 H1
Pinnocks Way. OX2 17 E3
Piper St. OX3 8 D5
Pipit Clo. OX4 21 F3
Pipkin Way. OX4 14 B3
Pitts Rd. OX3 9 F4
Pixey Pl. OX2 6 C3
Plantation Rd. OX2 13 E3
Plater Dri. OX2 12 D2
Playfield Rd. OX1 20 A4
Plough Clo. OX4 6 C3
Plover Dri. OX4 21 F3
Pochard Clo. OX4 21 G3
Polstead Rd. OX2 13 E1
Pond Clo. OX3 9 G4
Ponds La. OX3 7 H5
Pony Rd. OX4 15 F4
Poplar Gro. OX1 20 A3
Poplar Rd. OX2 17 G2
Portland Rd. OX2 7 E4
Pottery Piece. OX4 21 F2
Pottery Pl. OX4 21 F2
Pottle Clo. OX2 17 F1
Poulton Pl. OX4 21 G1
Poundfield Clo. OX3 9 F3
Preachers La. OX1 13 F6
Prestwich Pl. OX4 12 C5
Prichard Rd. OX3 8 B4
Primrose Pl. OX4 21 G2
Princes St. OX4 14 A1
Priors Forge. OX2 7 E2
Priory Rd. OX4 20 D2
Prunus Clo. OX4 21 G1
Pulker Clo. OX4 14 C5
Pullens Field. OX3 8 B5
Pullens La. OX3 8 B5
Purcell Rd. OX4 8 A4
Purland Clo. OX4 14 D4
Pusey La. OX1 3 C2
Pusey St. OX1 3 C2

Quarry High St. OX3 9 F5
Quarry Hollow. OX3 9 F5
Quarry Rd. OX3 9 F5
Quartermain Clo. OX4 14 B3
Queen St. OX1 3 C3
Queens Clo. OX1 17 F3
Queens La. OX1 3 E2

Radcliffe Rd. OX4 14 A4
Radford Clo. OX4 14 A6
Rahere Rd. OX4 14 D6
Railway La. OX4 20 C2
Raleigh Park Rd. OX2 17 H3
Rampion Clo. OX4 21 H2
Ramsay Rd. OX3 9 E4
Randolph St. OX4 14 A2
Rawlinson Rd. OX2 7 E6
Rawson Clo. OX4 6 C2
Raymund Rd. OX3 8 A3
Rectory Rd. OX4 14 A1
Red Copse La. OX1 18 D6
Red Lion Sq. OX1 3 C2
Rede Clo. OX3 9 E5
Redland Rd. OX3 8 C2
Redmoor Clo. OX4 20 D2

Redwood Clo. OX4 21 H2
Regent St. OX4 14 A2
Rest Harrow. OX4 21 H2
Rewley Rd. OX1 3 A2
Richards La. OX2 6 D4
Richmond Rd. OX1 3 B2
Rickyard Clo. OX1 3 A2
Riddell Pl. OX2 6 D2
Ridgefield Rd. OX4 14 B2
Ridgemont Clo. OX2 6 D4
Ridgeway. OX1 18 A6
Ridgeway Rd. OX4 9 F4
Ridley Rd. OX4 15 E3
Rimmer Clo. OX3 8 A2
Ringwood Rd. OX3 9 G4
Rippington Dri. OX3 8 A3
River Vw. OX1 20 A3
Rivermead Rd. OX4 14 A6
Riverside Ct. OX2 13 F6
Riverside Rd. OX2 12 C5
Robert Robinson Av. OX4 20 D3
Roberts Clo. OX3 9 G3
Robin Pl. OX4 21 F3
Rock Edge. OX3 9 E6
Rock Farm La. OX4 20 C3
*Roger Bacon La, Turn Again La. OX1 3 C4
Rogers St. OX2 7 E4
Rolfe Pl. OX3 8 B4
Roman Rd. OX33 11 G5
Roman Way. OX4 15 G4
Roosevelt Dri. OX3 8 C6
Rosamund Rd. OX2 6 B3
Rose Gdns. OX2 17 F2
Rose Hill. OX4 14 B5
Rose La. OX1 3 E3
Rose Pl. OX1 3 C4
Rossart Pl. OX2 16 C6
Rothafield Rd. OX2 6 C2
Routh Rd. OX3 9 G3
Rowan Gro. OX4 21 H2
Rowland Clo. OX2 6 B3
Rowles Clo. OX1 19 H6
Rowney Pl. OX4 14 B6
Rupert Rd. OX4 15 E3
Russell St. OX2 13 E5
Rutherway. OX2 12 D2
Rymers La. OX4 14 C4

Sage Walk. OX4 21 G3
St Aldates. OX1 3 C3
St Andrews La. OX3 8 D3
St Andrews Rd. OX3 8 D3
St Annes Rd. OX3 9 E5
St Barnabas St. OX2 3 A1
St Bernards Rd. OX2 13 E3
St Clements St. OX4 8 A6
St Cross Rd. OX1 3 E1
St Ebbes St. OX1 3 C3
St Georges Pl. OX1 3 C3
St Giles St. OX1 3 C1
St John St. OX1 3 B2
St Lawrence Rd. OX1 19 F3
St Leonards Rd. OX3 9 E5
St Lukes Rd. OX4 14 D5
St Margarets Rd. OX2 13 E2
St Martins Rd. OX4 14 B5
St Marys Clo. OX33 11 F4
St Marys Clo. OX4 20 D2
St Marys Rd. OX4 14 A2
St Michaels St. OX1 3 C2
St Nicholas Rd. OX 20 D2
St Omer Rd. OX4 14 D4
St Pauls Cres. OX2 17 G2
St Peters Rd. OX2 6 C3
St Swithuns Rd. OX1 20 A3
St Thomas St. OX1 3 A3
Salegate La. OX4 15 E4
Salford Rd. OX3 7 H6
Salisbury Cres. OX2 7 E3
Salter Clo. OX1 19 F1
Samphire Rd. OX4 21 G2
Sandfield Rd. OX3 8 C4
Sandford La. OX1 20 A5
Sandford Link Rd. OX4 20 D2
Sandford Rd. OX4 20 C3
Sandy La. OX4 18 A6
Sandy La. OX4 15 E6
Sandy La. OX4 14 D5
Sandy Lane West. OX4 21 E1
Saunders Rd. OX4 14 C5
Savile Rd. OX1 3 D2
Sawpit Rd. OX4 15 E4
Saxifrage Sq. OX4 21 G3
Saxon Way. OX3 8 C3

Scholar Pl. OX2 17 F3
School Ct. OX2 3 A1
School Pl. OX1 19 G2
Scott Rd. OX2 7 E3
Scrutton Clo. OX3 9 F4
Seacourt Rd. OX2 17 G2
Salesian Gdns. OX4 14 D3
Sermon Clo. OX3 9 G5
Setton Rd. OX3 9 E4
Seventh Av. OX4 15 F2
Shaftesbury Rd. OX3 9 E3
Sheepway Ct. OX4 14 B5
Sheldon Way. OX3 20 D1
Shelford Pl. OX3 9 E6
Shelley Rd. OX4 14 C3
Shelley Rd. OX3 9 E5
Shepherds Hill. OX4 21 G2
Sheriffs Dri. OX2 6 C3
Ship St. OX1 3 C3
Shirelake Clo. OX1 13 F6
Shoe La. OX1 3 C3
Shorte Clo. OX4 15 F2
Shotover Hill. OX3 9 G6
Silkdale Clo. OX4 14 D4
Silver Rd. OX4 14 B3
Simons Clo. OX33 11 F4
Simpsons Way. OX1 20 A4
*Skeyne Clo, Desmesne Furze. OX3 8 C6
Skylark Pl. OX4 21 E2
Slade Clo. OX3 9 E6
Slaymaker Clo. OX3 9 G5
Snowdon Mede. OX3 8 B3
Songers Clo. OX4 17 E3
Sorrel Rd. OX4 21 G1
South Croft. OX3 8 B1
South Parade. OX2 6 D4
South Parks Rd. OX1 3 D1
South St. OX2 12 D5
Southdale Rd. OX2 6 D2
Southern By-Pass. OX2 17 G2
Southern By-Pass Rd. OX1 19 F4
Southern By-Pass Rd Botley. OX2 18 C1
Southfield Pk. OX4 14 C5
Southfield Rd. OX4 14 B6
Southmoor Pl. OX2 13 E2
Southmoor Rd. OX2 13 E2
Sparrow Way. OX4 21 G3
Sparsey Pl. OX2 7 E2
Speedwell St. OX1 3 C4
Spencer Cres. OX4 14 B6
Spindleberry Clo. OX4 21 F2
Spinney Field. OX4 21 F3
Spooner Clo. OX3 9 F4
Spring Clo. OX3 19 F5
Spring La. OX4 21 E1
Spring La. OX3 9 F5
Spring La. OX33 10 A5
Springfield Rd. OX3 8 D4
Spruce Gdns. OX4 21 F3
Squitchey La. OX2 6 D3
Stable Clo. OX1 3 A3
Stainfield Rd. OX3 8 C3
Stainer Pl. OX3 8 A3
Stanley Clo. OX2 17 H2
Stanley Rd. OX4 14 A3
Stansfield Clo. OX3 9 F6
Stansfield Pl. OX3 9 F6
Stanton Rd. OX2 18 B2
Stanville Rd. OX2 17 F3
Stanway Rd. OX3 9 G4
Stapleton Rd. OX3 8 D5
Station Rd. OX33 11 F4
Staunton Rd. OX3 8 D3
Staverton Rd. OX2 7 E6
Steep Rise. OX3 8 C2
Stephen Rd. OX3 8 D4
Stewart St. OX1 19 F2
Stile Rd. OX3 9 E4
Stimpsons Clo. OX2 17 F2
Stockleys Rd. OX3 8 B2
Stockmore St. OX4 13 H6
Stoke Pl. OX3 8 D3
Stone Clo. OX2 17 F2
Stone Quarry La. OX4 14 B1
Stonor Pl. OX3 8 C2
Stowford Rd. OX3 9 F3
Stowood Clo. OX3 9 E4
Stratfield Rd. OX2 7 E4
Stratford St. OX4 14 A1
Stubble Clo. OX2 17 E3
Stubbs Av. OX3 15 F2

Sturges Clo. OX3 9 E3
Sugworth La. OX1 20 A6
Summerfield. OX1 19 G2
Summerfield Rd. OX2 7 E4
Summerhill Rd. OX2 6 D4
Sunderland Av. OX2 6 C2
Sundew Clo. OX4 21 H1
Sunningwell Rd. OX1 19 G2
*Sunny Rise,
 Gidley Way. OX33 10 B6
Sunnyside. OX4 15 E4
Sunnyside. OX33 11 G4
Sutton Rd. OX3 8 C2
Swan St. OX2 12 D5
Swallow Clo. OX4 21 H3
Swift Clo. OX4 21 H2
Sweetmans Rd. OX2 17 H3
Swinbourne Rd. OX4 20 D1
Swinburne Rd. OX4 14 A4
Sycamore Rd. OX2 17 G3

Tackley Pl. OX2 13 E2
Taggs Gate. OX3 9 F3
Talbot Rd. OX2 6 D1
Tarragon Dri. OX4 21 G3
Taverner Pl. OX3 8 A3
Tawney St. OX4 14 B1
Teal Clo. OX4 21 G3
Templar Rd. OX2 6 D2
Templars Clo. OX33 11 E4
Temple Rd. OX4 14 D4
Temple St. OX4 13 H6
Tern Walk. OX4 21 F3
Thackley End. OX2 7 E6
Thames St. OX1 3 B4
Thames View Rd. OX3 20 B1
The Avenue. OX1 20 A3
The Avenue. OX33 11 G5
The Beeches. OX3 9 E3
The Croft. OX3 8 D4
The Devils Backbone.
 OX1 19 F3
The Garth. OX2 17 H2
The Glebe. OX33 11 F4
The Grates. OX4 14 D5
The Hamel. OX1 3 B3
The Larches. OX3 9 G4
The Link,
 New Marston. OX3 8 A3
The Link,
 Risinghurst. OX3 9 G4
The New Walk. OX1 3 D4
The Oval. OX4S 20 B1
The Paddock. OX1 20 A5
The Paddox. OX2 6 D3
The Park. OX2 16 C6
The Plain. OX1 3 F4
The Ridings. OX3 9 G6
The Roundway. OX3 9 F4
The Slade. OX3 9 E6
The Stables. OX3 9 F5
The Triangle. OX33 11 G4
The Winnyards. OX2 16 C6
Third Acre Rise. OX2 17 F2
Thistle Dri. OX4 21 H1
Thomson Ter. OX4 20 C1
Thorncliffe Rd. OX2 7 E5
Three Corners Rd. OX4 21 H2
Three Fields Rd. OX3 15 F2
Thrift Pl. OX4 21 G2
Tidmarsh La. OX1 3 B3
Tilbury La. OX2 17 F1
Tilehouse Clo. OX3 9 F4
Timothy Way. OX4 21 H1
Titup Hall Dri. OX3 9 E6
Tonybee Clo. OX2 17 G3
Toot Hill Butts. OX3 9 F4
Town Furze. OX3 15 E2
Townsend Sq. OX4 14 A4
Trafford Rd. OX3 9 F4
Tree La. OX4 14 A5
Trefoil Pl. OX4 21 H1
Trevor Pl. OX4 14 C4
Trinity Pl. OX4 14 A3
Trinity Rd. OX4 9 F5
Trinity St. OX4 3 B4
Troy Clo. OX3 15 F2
Tucker Rd. OX4 21 F1
Tudor Clo. OX4 14 A5
Tumbledown Hill. OX2 16 B4
Turl St. OX1 3 D3
Turn Again La. OX1 3 C4
Turner Clo. OX4 14 D3
Turnpike Rd. OX4 17 F4
Tyndale Pl. OX33 11 G4
Tyndale Rd. OX4 13 H5

Ulfgar Rd. OX2 6 C3
Underhill Circus. OX3 9 F3
Union St. OX4 14 A1
Upland Park Rd. OX2 6 D3
Upper Fisher Row. OX1 3 B3
Upper Rd. OX1 19 G5
Upton Clo. OX4 20 D1
Upway Rd. OX3 8 C2

Valentia Rd. OX3 8 C5
*Valley Rd,
 Gidley Way. OX33 10 B6
Van Diemans La. OX4 14 D6
Venables Clo. OX2 3 A1
Verbena Way. OX4 21 F3
Vernon Av. OX2 18 B1
Vetch Pl. OX4 21 G1
Vicarage Clo. OX4 20 D2
Vicarage La. OX1 19 F2
Vicarage Rd. OX1 19 G2
Victor St. OX2 3 A1
Victoria Rd. OX2 7 E3
Villiers La. OX4 14 B5
Violet Way. OX4 21 F3

Walton Cres. OX1 3 B1
Walton La. OX1 3 B1
Walton Manor Ct. OX2 13 E3
Walton St. OX1 3 B1
Walton Well Rd. OX2 12 D3
Warbler Walk. OX4 21 F2
Warburg Cres. OX4 21 G1
Warnborough Rd. OX2 13 E2
Warneford La. OX3 8 C6
Warneford Rd. OX4 14 B2
Warren Cres. OX3 9 E6
Warwick St. OX4 14 A3
Water Eaton Rd. OX2 7 E3
Watermill Way. OX3 9 G3
Watlington Rd. OX4 15 F5
*Wayfaring Clo,
 Violet Way. OX4 21 F3
Wayneflete Rd. OX3 9 G3
Webbs Clo. OX2 6 A3
Weirs La. OX1 19 G3
Weldon Rd. OX3 8 A4
Wellington Pl. OX1 3 C2
Wellington Sq. OX1 3 B1
Wellington St. OX2 3 A1
Wentworth Rd. OX2 7 E3
Wesley Clo. OX4 21 G1
West St. OX2 12 D5
West Vw. OX4 14 B5
West Way. OX2 17 G2
Westbury Cres. OX4 14 C5
West Field Clo. OX4 14 C3
Western By-Pass,
 Botley. OX2 12 A1
Western By-Pass,
 Wolvercote. OX2 6 A3
Western Rd. OX1 19 F1
Westfield Rd. OX33 11 E4
Westlands Dri. OX3 8 C2
Westminster Way.
 OX2 17 G2
Westrup Clo. OX3 8 A4
Weyland Rd. OX3 9 E5
Wharton Rd. OX3 9 E4
*Wheatsheaf Yard,
 High St. OX1 3 D3
White Rd. OX4 15 E4
Whitehouse Rd. OX1 19 F1
Whitethorn Way. OX4 21 F2
Whitson Pl. OX4 14 B2
Wick Clo. OX3 9 E3
Wilberforce St. OX3 8 D5
Wilcote Rd. OX3 9 F3
Wilkins Rd. OX4 15 E4
William Kimber Cres.
 OX3 9 E4
William Orchard Clo.
 OX3 8 D3
William St. OX3 8 A5
Williamson Way. OX4 20 B1
Willow Way. OX4 21 F2
Wilmots. OX44 21 H6
Winchester Rd. OX2 13 F2
Windale Av. OX4 21 G2
Windmill La. OX33 10 D5
Windmill Rd. OX3 8 D4
Windsor Cres. OX3 7 H6
Windsor St. OX3 8 D5
Wingate Clo. OX4 21 F1
Wingfield St. OX4 14 A1
Wolsey Rd. OX2 7 E2
Wolvercote Grn. OX2 6 B3

Wood Farm Rd. OX3 9 F6
Woodbine Pl. OX1 3 A3
Woodhouse Way. OX4 14 B5
Woodlands Clo. OX3 8 C5
Woodlands Rd. OX3 8 C5
Woodpecker Grn. OX4 21 G3
Woodruff Clo. OX4 21 G1
Woodstock Clo. OX2 6 D3
Woodstock Rd,
 Jericho. OX2 3 A2
Woodstock Rd,
 Wolvercote. OX2 6 B1
Wooten Dri. OX4 14 B5
Worcester Pl. OX1 3 B2
Worcester St. OX1 3 B3
Wren Clo. OX33 11 F4
Wren Rd. OX2 7 E3
Wrightson Clo. OX33 10 B6
Wyatt Rd. OX2 7 E2
Wychwood La. OX3 9 G5
Wykeham Cres. OX4 14 C5
Wylie Clo. OX3 15 E1
Wynbush Rd. OX4 20 B1
Wyndham Way. OX2 6 D3
Wytham St. OX1 19 G2

Yarnells Hill. OX2 17 H3
Yarnells Rd. OX2 17 H2
Yarrow Clo. OX4 21 F3
Yeats Clo. OX4 15 F3
Yeftly Dri. OX4 20 B2
Yew Clo. OX4 21 H1
York Av. OX3 9 E6
York Pl. OX4 13 H5
York Rd. OX3 9 E5

## ABINGDON

Abbey Clo. OX14 23 E5
Abbott Rd. OX14 23 E5
Abingdon By-Pass.
 OX14 22 A6
Abingdon Rd,
 Culham. OX14 25 H4
Abingdon Rd,
 Drayton. OX14 24 B5
Alexander Clo. OX14 23 F1
All Saints La. OX14 25 G6
Allder Clo. OX14 22 D2
Amyce Clo. OX14 23 G2
Andersey Way. OX14 25 E2
Anna Pavlova Clo.
 OX14 23 G2
Appleford Dri. OX14 23 F2
Appleford Rd. OX14 25 G5
Argentan Clo. OX14 24 D2
Ashenden Clo. OX14 23 E4
Ashgate. OX14 24 D2
Ashmole Rd. OX14 25 E2
Aston Clo. OX14 22 D5
Audlett Dri. OX14 23 E5
Austin Pl. OX14 22 D3
Avon Rd. OX13 22 B2

Bailie Clo. OX14 25 E1
Baker Rd. OX14 25 E2
Ballard Chase. OX14 23 E1
Barfleur Clo. OX14 23 G2
Barrow Hill Clo. OX14 23 G3
Barrow Rd. OX13 22 A4
Barton La. OX14 23 F5
Bath St. OX14 22 D4
Beagle Clo. OX14 23 G2
Benson Rd. OX14 22 D3
Bergen Av. OX14 24 D2
Berry Croft. OX14 22 C4
Beverley Clo. OX14 22 D3
Blacklands Way. OX14 22 B5
Blacknall Rd. OX14 24 D1
Boreford Rd. OX14 23 F2
Borough Walk. OX14 22 D4
Bostock Rd. OX14 22 C6
Boulter Dri. OX14 23 E1
Bourlon Wood. OX14 22 C3
Bowgrave Copse.
 OX14 23 G3
Bowyer Rd. OX14 23 E4
Boxhill Rd. OX14 23 E4
Boxhill Walk. OX14 22 D4
Brampton Clo. OX14 22 C4
Bridge St. OX14 22 D5
Bridges Clo. OX14 24 C1
Broad St. OX14 22 D5

Brode Clo. OX14 23 F2
Brook St. OX14 25 F6
Brookside. OX14 23 E3
Bucklersbury Rd. OX14 23 F2
Burton Clo. OX14 24 C1
Bury St. OX14 22 D6
Buscot Dri. OX14 23 F3
Byron Clo. OX14 24 C1

Caldecott Clo. OX14 24 D1
Caldecott Rd. OX14 24 D1
Cameron Av. OX14 23 G3
Campion Rd. OX14 23 G4
Carse Clo. OX14 23 F2
Caudwell Clo. OX14 24 B5
Causeway. OX14 23 E6
Cemetery Rd. OX14 22 C5
Challenor Clo. OX14 25 E2
Champs Clo. OX14 23 G3
Chandlers Clo. OX14 23 G3
Chapel La. OX14 25 F6
Charney Av. OX14 23 G2
Chaunterell Way. OX14 24 C1
*Checker Wk,
 Abbey Clo. OX14 23 E6
Cheers Farm. OX14 24 C6
Cherry Tree Dri. OX13 22 B3
Cherwell Clo. OX14 23 F4
Chestnut Tree Clo.
 OX13 22 B3
Chiers Dri. OX14 24 C6
Childrey Way. OX14 23 F2
Chilton Clo. OX14 23 F3
Cholswell Rd. OX13 22 B1
Church La. OX14 24 B5
Church St. OX14 25 F6
Churchmere Rd. OX14 25 G6
Clarendon Clo. OX14 23 G5
Clevelands. OX14 23 E4
Clifton Dri. OX14 22 D5
Coleridge Dri. OX14 24 C2
Collingwood Clo. OX14 22 D4
Colwell Dri. OX14 22 B5
Compton Dri. OX14 23 F2
Conduit Rd. OX14 22 D6
Conway Rd. OX13 22 B2
Copenhagen Dri. OX14 22 B4
Corn Avill Clo. OX14 23 G3
Corneville Rd. OX14 24 B5
Coromandel. OX14 24 D2
Covent Clo. OX14 24 D2
Crabtree La. OX14 24 B5
Crabtree Pl. OX14 23 F5
Creney Walk. OX14 22 D4
Croasdell Clo. OX14 24 D2
Crosslands Dri. OX14 22 C3
Crown Mews. OX14 22 D6
Culham Clo. OX14 23 F3
Cullerne Clo. OX14 23 E2
Curtis Av. OX14 23 F5
Curtyn Clo. OX14 22 C4

Daisy Bank. OX14 23 G4
Darrell Way. OX14 22 D4
Dart Rd. OX13 22 B2
Dearlove Clo. OX14 22 D3
Denton Clo. OX14 23 F5
Derwent Clo. OX13 22 B2
Dobson Ct. OX14 23 E5
Dorchester Cres. OX14 23 F3
Drayton East Way.
 OX14 24 B6
Drayton Rd,
 Drayton. OX14 24 C6
Drayton Rd,
 Sutton Wick. OX14 24 B4
Duffield Clo. OX14 23 F3
Dundas Clo. OX14 23 F5
Dunmore Rd. OX14 22 C3

Eason Dri. OX14 23 G4
East St Helen St. OX14 22 D6
Eastway. OX14 24 B6
Eden Croft. OX14 23 F2
Edward St. OX14 22 C6
Eldridge Clo. OX14 22 D2
Elizabeth Av. OX14 23 G2
Elm Tree Walk. OX13 22 A3
Elwes Clo. OX14 23 F5
Ely Clo. OX14 24 C1
Ethelhem Clo. OX14 23 G3
Eney Clo. OX14 23 G3
Evelin Rd. OX14 22 C3
Evenlode Pk. OX14 23 G3
Exbourne Rd. OX14 22 C6
Eyston Way. OX14 22 B6

Fairacres. OX14 22 B6
Fairfield Pl. OX14 22 D4
Faringdon Rd. OX14 22 D5
Farm Rd. OX14 22 D2
Farriers Mews. OX14 23 E5
Fennel Way. OX14 23 G4
Ferguson Pl. OX14 23 G5
Ferry Walk. OX14 25 E1
Fieldside. OX14 22 C3
Finmore Clo. OX14 22 D4
Fisher Clo. OX14 24 A5
Fishermans Wharf.
 OX14 25 E2
Fitzharrys Rd. OX14 22 D2
Foster Rd. OX14 22 D2
Foxborough Rd. OX14 23 H3
Francis Little Dri. OX14 24 C1
Franklyn Clo. OX14 23 E2
Fullwell Clo. OX14 22 C3

Gainsborough Grn.
 OX14 24 D1
Gall Clo. OX14 23 G5
Galley Field. OX14 23 F4
Gardiner Clo. OX14 23 F3
Garford Clo. OX14 23 F3
Geoffrey Barbour Rd.
 OX14 23 E4
Gibson Clo. OX14 23 E2
Ginge Clo. OX14 23 G2
Glyme Clo. OX14 23 F3
Godfrey Clo. OX14 24 D1
Godwyn Clo. OX14 22 D5
Golafre Rd. OX14 23 E3
Gordon Dri. OX14 23 G3
Gravel La. OX14 24 B5
Grebe Clo. OX14 25 E2
Greenacres. OX14 23 B4
Grundy Clo. OX14 23 F4

Halls Clo. OX14 24 B6
Hadland Rd. OX14 23 G4
Hamble Dri. OX14 23 G3
Hanson Rd. OX14 22 D2
Harcourt Way. OX14 24 C4
Harding Rd. OX14 22 C4
Hart Clo. OX14 23 G5
Harwell Clo. OX14 23 F3
Hawthorne Av. OX13 22 A3
Healey Clo. OX14 24 D1
Hean Clo. OX14 23 F2
Heathcote Pl. OX14 23 G4
Hedgemead Av. OX14 23 G3
Hendred Way. OX14 23 F3
Henleys La. OX14 24 B5
Henor Mill Clo. OX14 23 F5
Herman Clo. OX14 23 F5
Hermitage Rd. OX14 24 D1
Herons Walk. OX14 22 D4
High St,
 Abingdon. OX14 22 D6
High St,
 Culham. OX14 25 G4
High St, Sutton
 Courtenay. OX14 25 F6
Hilliat Fields. OX14 24 B5
Hillview Rd. OX14 22 D3
*Hive Mews,
 West St. OX14 22 D6
Hobbs Clo. OX14 23 F5
Hogarth Pl. OX14 25 E1
Holland Rd. OX14 23 E3
Holywell Clo. OX14 23 G2
Hound Clo. OX14 23 G3
Hunter Clo. OX14 23 F2
Hyde Pl. OX14 24 D2

INDUSTRIAL & RETAIL:
Abingdon Business Pk.
 OX14 22 B5
Abingdon Science Pk.
 OX14 23 G5
Drayton Rd Trading Est.
 OX14 24 C1
Fairacres Retail Pk.
 OX14 22 A6
Radley Rd Ind Est.
 OX14 23 F4
Thames View Ind Pk.
 OX14 23 F3
Inkerman Clo. OX14 22 C4
Isis Clo. OX14 23 G3
Jackman Clo. OX14 23 E5

John Mason Rd. OX14 23 E4
John Morris Rd. OX14 25 E1

Kempster Clo. OX14 23 F5
Kennet Rd. OX14 23 F3
Kensington Clo. OX14 24 D2
Kent Clo. OX14 23 G5
Kestrel Rd. OX13 22 A3
Kimber Rd. OX14 22 A6
Kingfisher Clo. OX14 25 E2
Kingston Clo. OX14 22 D5
Knapp Clo. OX14 22 C4
Knollys Clo. OX14 23 E1
Kysbie Clo. OX14 22 D2

Laburnum Av. OX13 22 B3
Ladygrove Paddock.
  OX14 24 D1
Lambrick Way. OX14 25 E2
Lammas Clo. OX14 23 E4
Langley Rd. OX14 22 D2
Larkhill Rd. OX14 22 C4
Larkhill Pl. OX14 22 C4
Lee Av. OX14 23 F5
Lely Ct. OX14 25 E2
Lenthall Rd. OX14 22 D4
Letcombe Av. OX14 22 D5
Levery Clo. OX14 23 G4
Lindsay Dri. OX14 23 F3
Lockway. OX14 24 A6
Loddon Clo. OX14 23 F3
Lombard St. OX14 22 D6
Long Furlong Rd. OX13 22 C1
Long Tow. OX14 22 B2
Longfellow Dri. OX14 24 C1
Longmead. OX14 22 C4
Lovelace Clo. OX14 23 E2
Loyd Clo. OX14 23 E2
Lucca Dri. OX14 24 C2
Lumberd Rd. OX14 23 F2
Lyford Rd. OX14 24 A5
Lyford Way. OX14 23 F2
Lynges Clo. OX14 23 G2
Lyon Clo. OX14 23 E3

Maberley Clo. OX14 24 C1
Magnette Clo. OX14 23 E5
Mandeville Clo. OX14 23 E2
Manor Clo. OX14 24 B5
Marcham Rd,
  Abingdon. OX14 22 A6
Marcham Rd,
  Drayton. OX14 24 B6
Market Pl. OX14 23 E6
Marsh Ct. OX14 22 D4
Masefield Cres. OX14 24 C1
Mattock Way. OX14 23 F2
Mayotts Rd. OX14 22 C6
Meadowside. OX14 22 C6
Meadowside Ct,
  Meadowside. OX14 22 C6
Meads Clo. OX14 24 B5
Medlicott Dri. OX14 24 C1
Medway Clo. OX14 22 B1
Medway Rd. OX13 22 B1
Merlin Rd. OX13 22 A3
Metcalfe Clo. OX14 24 D3
Midget Clo. OX14 24 D2
Mill La. OX14 22 D6
Mill Paddock. OX14 22 D6
Mill Rd. OX14 24 C1
Minchins Clo. OX14 23 G4
Mons Way. OX14 22 C4
Morton Clo. OX14 23 G5
Mullard Way. OX14 22 C6

Napier Ct. OX14 23 F5
Nash Dri. OX14 24 C1
Nene Rd. OX13 22 B2
New St. OX14 23 E5
Newman La. OX14 24 B4
Norbrook Clo. OX14 23 G2
Norman Av. OX14 23 E4
Norris Clo. OX14 23 G3
North Av. OX14 23 E2
North Quay. OX14 25 E2
Northcourt La. OX14 23 E3
Northcourt Rd. OX14 22 D4
Northcourt Walk. OX14 23 E4
Northfield Rd. OX14 23 F2
Nufield Way. OX14 22 A5
Nuneham Sq. OX14 22 D5
Nyatt Rd. OX14 23 G5

Ock Mill Clo. OX14 22 C6
Ock St. OX14 22 C6

Old Farm Clo. OX14 23 G5
Old Station Yd. OX14 23 E5
Orchard Clo. OX14 23 E4
Orpwood Way. OX14 24 C1
Otwell Clo. OX14 23 F2
Overmead. OX14 24 D2
Oxford Rd. OX14 23 E5

Pagisters Rd. OX14 23 G3
Park Cres. OX14 22 C5
Park Rd. OX14 22 C6
Peachcroft Rd. OX14 23 G2
Pearsons Mead. OX14 22 D3
Peep-o-Day La. OX14 25 E5
Penn Clo. OX14 23 G2
Picklers Hill. OX14 23 E3
Potenger Way. OX14 22 C6
Preston Rd. OX14 24 C2
Prince Gro. OX14 23 E1
Pudsey Clo. OX14 24 D2
Purslane. OX14 23 G4
Pykes Clo. OX14 23 F2
Pytenry Clo. OX14 23 F2

Queen St. OX14 22 D6

Radley Rd. OX14 23 E5
Rainbow Way. OX14 23 F2
Ramsons Way. OX14 23 G4
Rawlings Gro. OX14 22 C4
Reade Av. OX14 23 G5
Reynolds Way. OX14 25 E1
Riley Clo. OX14 24 D1
Ripington Ct. OX14 24 B4
River Clo. OX14 25 E2
Rivy Clo. OX14 23 G4
Rookery Clo. OX13 22 A3
Rose Av. OX14 23 E1
Rushmead Copse.
  OX14 23 G2
Ruskin Av. OX14 25 E2
Rutherford Clo. OX14 23 F4

Saddlers Ct. OX14 23 F2
Saffron Ct. OX14 23 G4
St Amand Dri. OX14 25 E1
St Andrews Clo. OX14 23 G2
St Edmunds La. OX14 22 D6
St Helens Ct. OX14 22 D6
*St Helens Mews, West
  St Helen St. OX14 22 D6
St Helens Wharf. OX14 22 D6
St Johns Rd. OX14 23 E4
St Marys Grn. OX14 22 D4
St Michaels Av. OX14 22 C6
St Nicholas Gr. OX14 22 D4
St Peters Rd. OX14 23 G3
Sandford Clo. OX14 23 G2
Saxton Rd. OX14 24 D1
Schongau La. OX14 23 E3
Sellwood Rd. OX14 23 E3
Severn Rd. OX13 22 B2
Sewell Clo. OX14 23 G4
Shelley Clo. OX14 23 E3
Shepherd Gdns. OX14 24 C1
Sherwood Av. OX14 23 F5
Shrives Clo. OX14 23 F2
Sint Niklaas Clo. OX14 24 D2
Solafre Rd. OX14 25 E1
South Av. OX14 23 E2
Southmoor Way. OX14 22 C4
Spenlove Clo. OX14 22 D2
Spey Rd. OX13 22 B1
Spring Gdns. OX14 22 C5
Spring Rd. OX14 22 C6
Springfield Dri. OX14 22 C4
Stanford Dri. OX14 22 D5
Stenton Clo. OX14 25 E2
Stert St. OX14 23 E6
Stevenson Dri. OX14 24 C4
Stevenson Rd. OX14 24 A6
Stockey End. OX14 23 G2
Stonehill La. OX14 24 C3
Stonehill Walk. OX14 24 D2
Stratton Way. OX14 22 D6
Suffolk Way. OX14 24 D1
Summer Field. OX14 23 E3
Sunningwell Rd. OX13 22 C1
Sutton Clo. OX14 22 D5
Sutton Wick La. OX14 24 B4
Swinburne Rd. OX14 23 E4
Sycamore Clo. OX13 22 A3
Sympson Clo. OX14 24 D1

Tatham Rd. OX14 23 E4
Tennyson Dri. OX14 24 C1

Terrington Clo. OX14 23 E3
Thames St. OX14 23 E6
Thames View. OX14 23 E5
The Burycroft. OX14 25 F3
The Chestnuts. OX14 23 G3
The Copse. OX14 23 G3
The Court. OX14 22 C3
The Glebe. OX14 25 G4
The Grove. OX14 23 F2
The Holt. OX14 23 E5
The Hyde. OX14 24 D2
The Motte. OX14 23 E5
The Pentagon. OX14 23 G5
The Quadrant. OX14 23 F5
The Spinney. OX14 22 C4
The Warren. OX14 23 F5
Thesiger Rd. OX14 23 E5
Thistlecroft Clo. OX14 23 F2
Thornehill Walk. OX14 22 D4
Thrupp La. OX14 23 H4
Thurston Clo. OX14 22 D6
Tollgate Rd. OX14 25 H4
Tower Clo. OX14 22 C6
Townsend. OX14 25 E2
Trendell Pl. OX14 22 D4
Trinity Clo. OX14 23 F2
Turberville Clo. OX14 25 E1
Turnagain La. OX14 23 E6
Turner Rd. OX14 24 D2
Twelve Acre Dri. OX14 23 F1
Tyne Rd. OX14 22 B2

Upton Clo. OX14 23 F3

Victoria Rd. OX14 22 C6
Villeboys Clo. OX14 23 G4
Vineyard. OX14 23 E5
Virginia Way. OX14 24 C2

Wallace Clo. OX14 23 G2
Warwick Clo. OX14 23 E4
Waxes Clo. OX14 23 G3
Welford Gdns. OX14 23 F3
Welland Clo. OX13 22 B2
Wellesbourne Clo.
  OX14 23 F5
West Av. OX14 23 F5
West Quay. OX14 25 E3
West St Helen St.
  OX14 22 D6
Westfields. OX14 22 C5
Wharf Clo. OX14 25 E1
Wheatcroft Clo. OX14 23 E2
Whitecross. OX13 22 C1
Whitehorns Way.
  OX14 24 A6
Whitehouse Clo. OX13 22 B3
Whitelock Rd. OX14 23 E4
Whites La. OX14 23 H2
Wick Clo. OX14 23 G2
Wildmoor Gate. OX14 22 C4
Willow Brook. OX14 22 B5
Willow Tree Clo. OX14 22 A3
Wilsham Rd. OX14 25 E1
Windrush Ct. OX14 22 B5
Windrush Way. OX14 23 F3
Winsmore La. OX14 22 D6
Winterbourne Rd.
  OX14 22 C6
Withington Clo. OX14 22 D5
Woodcote Way. OX14 24 D2
Woodley Clo. OX14 23 E2
Wootton Rd. OX14 22 C1
Wordsworth Rd. OX14 24 C1
Wyndyke Furlong.
  OX14 22 B4

Yeld Hall Rd. OX14 23 G2
Yew Tree Mews. OX14 22 D5
Ypres Way. OX14 22 C4

## EYNSHAM

Abbey Pl. OX8 26 C3
Abbey St. OX8 26 C2
Acre End St. OX8 26 B2
Back La. OX8 26 B2
Bartholomew Ct. OX8 26 B2
Beech Rd. OX8 26 C1
Blankstone Rd. OX8 26 B2
Cassington Rd. OX8 26 D1
Cheltenham Rd. OX8 26 A1
Chilbridge Rd. OX8 26 A3
Clover Pl. OX8 26 B2

Conduit La. OX8 26 C2
Cuckoo La. OX8 26 A1
Dovehouse Clo. OX8 26 C1
Duncan Clo. OX8 26 B1
Evans Clo. OX8 26 C2
Evans Rd. OX8 26 C2
Falstaff Clo. OX8 26 B2
Fruitlands. OX8 26 A1
Greens Rd. OX8 26 B1
Hanborough Clo. OX8 26 C1
Hanborough Rd. OX8 26 C1
Hawthorn Rd. OX8 26 C2
Heycroft. OX8 26 C3
High St. OX8 26 C2
**INDUSTRIAL & RETAIL:**
  Oakfield Ind Est.
  OX8 26 C3
John Lopes Rd. OX8 26 C2
Lombard St. OX8 26 C2
Marlborough Clo. OX8 26 C1
Marlborough Pl. OX8 26 C1
Mead La. OX8 26 D2
Merton Clo. OX8 26 B2
Mill St. OX8 26 C2
Mill St Mews. OX8 26 C2
Millmoor Cres. OX8 26 C1
Newland Clo. OX8 26 B2
Newland St. OX8 26 C2
Old Whitney Rd. OX8 26 A1
Orchard Clo. OX8 26 C2
Oxford Rd. OX8 26 C2
Pelican Pl. OX8 26 C1
Pinkhill La. OX8 26 B3
Queen St. OX8 26 C2
Queens Clo. OX8 26 C2
Queens La. OX8 26 C2
Shakespeare Rd. OX8 26 B1
Spareacre La. OX8 26 B1
Station Rd. OX8 26 B3
Stratford Dri. OX8 26 B1
Swan St. OX8 26 C2
Tanner La. OX8 26 C2
Thames St. OX8 26 C2
The Bitterell. OX8 26 C2
The Square. OX8 26 C2
Thornbury Clo. OX8 26 B2
Tilgarsley Rd. OX8 26 B1
Wharf Rd. OX8 26 D3
Whitney Rd. OX8 26 B1
Willows Edge. OX8 26 B2
Wytham Clo. OX8 26 C1
Wytham View. OX8 26 C1

## KIDLINGTON/
## YARNTON

Almond Av. OX5 5 F4
Andersons Clo. OX5 5 E3
App Rd. OX5 5 F3
Asa Clo. OX5 5 G4
Astley Av. OX5 5 G5
Axtel Clo. OX5 5 E2
Aysgarth Rd. OX5 4 C5
Azalea Av. OX5 5 G5
Banbury Rd. OX5 5 E1
Bankside. OX5 4 D1
Barn Clo. OX5 5 E3
Bartholomew Clo. OX5 4 C6
Basset Way. OX5 5 G2
Beagles Clo. OX5 5 H4
Beaufort Clo. OX5 5 F2
Beech Cres. OX5 5 F5
Begbroke Cres. OX5 4 C2
Begbroke Rd. OX5 4 B2
Belgrove Clo. OX5 5 F3
Bellenger Way. OX5 5 E3
Ben Clo. OX5 5 F2
Benmead Rd. OX5 5 F2
Bernard Clo. OX5 4 D6
Bicester Rd. OX5 5 G4
Blandford Rd. OX5 5 E1
Blenheim Rd. OX5 5 G3
Bowerman Clo. OX5 5 F3
Brandon Clo. OX5 5 E3
Brasenose Dri. OX5 5 G2
Briar Clo. OX5 5 E1
Briar End. OX5 5 E1
Broad Clo. OX5 5 F3
Buckland Ct. OX5 5 G4
Calves Clo. OX5 4 D6
Cassington La. OX5 4 D6
Cassington Rd. OX5 4 C6
Chamberlain Pl. OX5 5 E2
Charlbury Clo. OX5 5 E1

Cherry Clo. OX5 5 F4
Cherwell Av. OX5 5 G3
Chorefields. OX5 5 E2
Church La. OX5 4 C6
Church St. OX5 5 G2
Churchill Rd. OX5 5 F4
Cleveland Clo. OX5 5 H4
Copthorne Rd. OX5 5 F5
Cots Grn. OX5 5 E2
Court Clo. OX5 5 F3
Croft Av. OX5 5 G3
Cromwell Way. OX5 5 G5
Croxford Gdns. OX5 5 F5
Crown Rd. OX5 5 F2
Curtis Pl. OX5 5 F2
Curtis Rd. OX5 5 F2
Dale Pl. OX5 5 F2
Dashwood Av. OX5 4 C6
Dolton Clo. OX5 4 A3
Dukes Rd. OX5 5 G3
Edinburgh Dri. OX5 5 H3
Elm Gro. OX5 5 G5
Evans Ct. OX5 5 G3
Evans La. OX5 5 G3
Evenlode Cres. OX5 4 C1
Exeter Rd. OX5 5 F2
Fairfax Rd. OX5 5 G5
Farm Clo. OX5 5 G1
Fernhill Clo. OX5 5 E3
Fernhill Rd. OX5 4 B3
Field Clo,
  Kidlington. OX5 5 G3
Field Clo,
  Yarnton. OX5 4 C5
Flatford Pl. OX5 5 E1
Fletcher Clo. OX5 4 C6
Florence Clo OX5 5 G3
Follets Way. OX5 4 D6
Foxdown Clo. OX5 5 F2
Foxglove Rd. OX5 4 C3
Franklin Clo. OX5 5 G2
Freeborn Clo. OX5 5 G1
Frieze Way. OX5 5 G6
Frogwelldown La. OX5 4 A5
Gosford Clo. OX5 5 G5
Gravel Pits La. OX5 4 C5
Great Close Rd. OX5 4 D6
Green Rd. OX5 5 F3
Greystones Ct. OX5 5 E2
Grovelands. OX5 5 E3
Hampden Dri. OX5 5 G5
Hardwick Av. OX5 5 F4
Harts Clo. OX5 5 E3
Hawthorn Way. OX5 5 F4
Hazel Broadway. OX5 5 G5
Hazel Cres. OX5 5 F5
Helwys Pl. OX5 5 F1
Heyford Mead. OX5 5 E3
High St. OX5 5 F4
Holly Clo. OX5 5 F4
Home Clo. OX5 5 F2
Honor Clo. OX5 5 G3
**INDUSTRIAL & RETAIL:**
  Cherwell Business Centre.
  OX5 4 D1
  Kidlington Business Pk.
  OX5 4 D1
  Station Field Ind Est.
  OX5 4 D1
Judges Clo. OX5 5 F3
Kings Way Dri. OX5 5 H3
Laburnum Cres. OX5 5 F4
Lambs Clo. OX5 5 F1
Lane Clo. OX5 5 E3
Langford La. OX5 4 B1
Lee Clo. OX5 5 E3
Lincraft Clo. OX5 5 F4
Little Blenheim. OX5 4 C6
Lock Cres. OX5 5 F5
Lovelace Dri. OX5 5 H3
Lyne Rd. OX5 5 E2
Magnolia Clo. OX5 5 F4
Manor Way. OX5 5 G1
Maple Av. OX5 5 G4
Maple Ct. OX5 5 G4
Marlborough Av. OX5 5 E1
Marlborough Clo. OX5 5 E1
Marsh Clo. OX5 4 D6
Mead Way. OX5 5 F1
Meadow View. OX5 5 F1
Meadow Way. OX5 4 D6
Merton Way. OX5 4 C6
Mill End. OX5 5 H2
Mill St. OX5 5 G2
Morrell Clo. OX5 5 E3
Morton Av. OX5 5 F3

| Street | Ref | Street | Ref | Street | Ref |
|---|---|---|---|---|---|
| Morton Clo. OX5 | 5 F3 | Sandy La. OX5 | 4 C4 | Treeground Pl. OX5 | 5 F3 |
| Mulcaster Av. OX5 | 5 G3 | School Rd. OX5 | 5 G2 | Vicarage Rd. OX5 | 5 G2 |
| Newport Clo. OX5 | 5 F4 | Scott Clo. OX5 | 5 E3 | Water Eaton La. OX5 | 5 H4 |
| Nurseries Rd. OX5 | 5 F3 | South Av. OX5 | 5 G5 | Watermead. OX5 | 5 H2 |
| Oak Dri. OX5 | 5 G2 | South Clo. OX5 | 5 G5 | Watts Way. OX5 | 5 F2 |
| Old Chapel Pl. OX5 | 5 G2 | Spencer Av. OX5 | 4 C6 | Waverley Av. OX5 | 5 G3 |
| Orchard Way. OX5 | 5 G3 | Spindlers. OX5 | 5 G2 | Webbs Way. OX5 | 5 G2 |
| Osbourne Clo. OX5 | 5 E4 | Spring Hill Rd. OX5 | 4 A3 | White Way. OX5 | 5 F3 |
| Oxford Rd. OX5 | 5 F3 | Springfield Rd. OX5 | 5 G3 | Willow Clo. OX5 | 4 C5 |
| Park Av. OX5 | 5 E1 | Spruce Rd. OX5 | 5 F4 | Willow Way. OX5 | 4 C2 |
| Park Clo. OX5 | 4 C6 | Station App. OX5 | 4 D1 | Wilsdon Way. OX5 | 5 E2 |
| Partridge Pl. OX5 | 5 E2 | Sterling Clo. OX5 | 5 F2 | Winston Clo. OX5 | 5 F4 |
| Petre Pl. OX5 | 5 G2 | Sterling Rd. OX5 | 5 F2 | Wise Av. OX5 | 5 F2 |
| Ploughley Clo. OX5 | 5 E3 | Stocks Tree Clo. OX5 | 4 C6 | Wolsey Ct. OX5 | 4 A1 |
| Poplar Clo. OX5 | 5 G4 | Stoutsfield Clo. OX5 | 4 C6 | Woodstock Rd. OX5 | 4 A1 |
| Pound Clo. OX5 | 4 C6 | Stratfield Rd. OX5 | 5 F5 | Yarnton Ct. OX5 | 5 F3 |
| Prestide Pl. OX5 | 5 G3 | The Boulevard. OX5 | 4 C1 | Yarnton La. OX5 | 5 E5 |
| Quarry End. OX5 | 4 C3 | The Closes. OX5 | 5 F2 | Yarnton Rd. OX5 | 5 F4 |
| Queens Av. OX5 | 5 H3 | The Garth. OX5 | 4 C5 | | |
| Rosamund Way. OX5 | 4 D1 | The Homestead. OX5 | 5 E3 | **WOODSTOCK** | |
| Roundham Clo. OX5 | 5 E3 | The Moorlands. OX5 | 5 F1 | | |
| Rowan Clo. OX5 | 5 F4 | The Moors. OX5 | 5 E1 | | |
| Rowel Dri. OX5 | 4 C2 | The Paddocks. OX5 | 4 C6 | | |
| Rutten La. OX5 | 4 C5 | The Phelps. OX5 | 5 E3 | Banbury Rd. OX20 | 26 C5 |
| Rutters Clo. OX5 | 5 E3 | The Ridings. OX5 | 5 E2 | Bear Clo. OX20 | 26 C5 |
| St Johns Dri. OX5 | 5 G2 | The Rookery. OX5 | 5 E3 | Boundary Clo. OX20 | 26 C5 |
| St Marys Clo. OX5 | 5 G1 | The Spears. OX5 | 4 C5 | Briar Thicket. OX20 | 26 C5 |
| St Michaels La. OX5 | 4 B3 | Thorne Clo. OX5 | 5 E2 | Brook Hill. OX20 | 26 B5 |
| Sandhill Rd. OX5 | 4 C2 | Town Grn. OX5 | 5 G2 | Budds Clo. OX20 | 26 D4 |

| Street | Ref | Street | Ref |
|---|---|---|---|
| Cadogan Park. OX20 | 26 C5 | Parkside. OX20 | 26 C5 |
| Campbells Clo. OX20 | 26 C5 | Plane Tree Way. OX20 | 26 D5 |
| Churchill Clo. OX20 | 26 C5 | Princes Ride. OX20 | 26 C6 |
| Churchill Gate. OX20 | 26 C6 | Recreation Rd. OX20 | 26 C5 |
| Cockpit Clo. OX20 | 26 B5 | Rectory La. OX20 | 26 B5 |
| Crecy Walk. OX20 | 26 C6 | Rosamund Dri. OX20 | 26 A4 |
| Farm End. OX20 | 26 A4 | Shipton Rd. OX20 | 26 C5 |
| Flemings Rd. OX20 | 26 D5 | The Covert. OX20 | 26 C6 |
| Glovers Clo. OX20 | 26 C5 | The Ley. OX20 | 26 C5 |
| Glyme Clo. OX20 | 26 B4 | The Quadrangle. OX20 | 26 C4 |
| Green La. OX20 | 26 C4 | Union St. OX20 | 26 B5 |
| Harrisons La. OX20 | 26 B5 | Upper Brook Hill. OX20 | |
| Hedge End. OX20 | 26 C6 | Vanburgh Clo. OX20 | 26 B4 |
| Hensington Clo. OX20 | 26 D5 | Vermont Dri. OX20 | 26 A4 |
| Hensington Rd. OX20 | 26 B5 | Westland Way. OX20 | 26 A4 |
| High St. OX20 | 26 B5 | | |
| Hill Rise. OX20 | 26 A4 | | |
| Kerwood Clo. OX20 | 26 C5 | | |
| Manor Clo. OX20 | 26 B4 | | |
| Manor Rd. OX20 | 26 A4 | | |
| Market St. OX20 | 26 B5 | | |
| Marlborough Cres. OX20 | 26 B4 | | |
| Meadow Walk. OX20 | 26 C5 | | |
| New Rd. OX20 | 26 B5 | | |
| Oxford Rd. OX20 | 26 B5 | | |
| Oxford St. OX20 | 26 B5 | | |
| Park La. OX20 | 26 B5 | | |
| Park St. OX20 | 26 B5 | | |